ANTHOLOGY
of SONGS
for the
SOLO VOICE

ANTHOLOGY
of SONGS
for the
SOLO VOICE

EDITED AND ANNOTATED BY

Kenneth E. Miller
University of Missouri, St. Louis

Prentice Hall, *Englewood Cliffs, New Jersey 07632*

Library of Congress Cataloging-in-Publication Data

Anthology of songs for the solo voice / edited and annotated by
Kenneth E. Miller.
   1 score.
   Collection of 40 songs for medium high and medium low voice and piano, for beginning
students as well as for the experienced singer; includes a variety
of periods and types, from folk song to opera.
   Words in original languages (English, French, German, Italian, and
Latin) with English translations.
   ISBN 0-13-720558-9
   1. Songs (Medium high and medium low voice) with piano.   I. Miller, Kenneth E. (date)
   M1619.A727   1994   93-40691
                                                                                   CIP
                                                                                     M

Acquisitions editor: Bud Therien
Production editor and interior design: Hilda Tauber
Production coordinator: Bob Anderson
Cover design: Maureen Eide

 ©1994 by Prentice-Hall, Inc.
A Paramount Communications Company
Englewood Cliffs, New Jersey 07632

All English translations marked with an asterisk are from
English Singing Translations of Foreign Language Art Songs,
by the National Association of Teachers of Singing, 1976. Used by permission.

Printed in the United States of America
10 9 8 7 6 5 4 3 2 1

ISBN 0-13-720558-9

Prentice-Hall International (UK) Limited, *London*
Prentice-Hall of Australia Pty. Limited, *Sydney*
Prentice-Hall Canada Inc., *Toronto*
Prentice-Hall Hispanoamericana, S.A., *Mexico*
Prentice-Hall of India Private Limited, *New Delhi*
Prentice-Hall of Japan, Inc., *Tokyo*
Simon & Schuster Asia Pte. Ltd., *Singapore*
Editora Prentice-Hall do Brasil, Ltda., *Rio de Janeiro*

Contents

FRENCH SONGS

LATIN SONGS

Preface

Anthology of Songs for the Solo Voice is a well-rounded and varied collection of songs for beginning students as well as singers with more experience who seek to expand their repertory. It has been compiled after consultation with numerous faculty members and voice teachers, and their contribution in helping to choose the repertory is gratefully acknowledged.

The volume contains 40 songs, each of which is printed in a medium high and a medium low key so that the singer can choose the range best suited to a particular voice. The voice range is designated on the title page of each song, and considerable attention has also been given to tessitura.

Music of various periods and traditions is included, from American folk songs to operatic arias. The texts are in English, French, German, Italian, and Latin. Pertinent information about the composers and suggestions for interpretation of the music are given in Appendix A. The foreign language texts have been transcribed in accordance with the International Phonetic Alphabet. A pronunciation chart of the IPA symbols used in the transcriptions is provided in Appendix B.

Beginning students will benefit from consuming the information found in Miller, *Principles of Singing,* 2nd edition, which provides a solid foundation for the development of vocal technique. However, some studio voice teachers prefer to impart all vocal instruction themselves, and such teaching circumstances may be beneficial for some students. Since many of these songs and arias have been considered important to the vocal and musical development of students over a period of many years, the information contained here will be valuable to the development of singers whether in a voice class, in a studio, or in a diction/repertory class.

The author wishes to extend a word of gratitude to all those students and teachers who have contributed toward the completion of the manuscript. Thanks are also due the professional staff at Prentice Hall who contributed generously of their own expertise.

Kenneth E. Miller
St. Louis, Missouri

HAVE YOU SEEN BUT A WHITE LILLIE GROW

MEDIUM HIGH VOICE

Ben Jonson

Anonymous
ed. KEM

Have you seen but a white[1] lil-lie grow _____ be-

fore rude hands had touch'd it; Have you mark'd _ but _ the _ fall of the snow

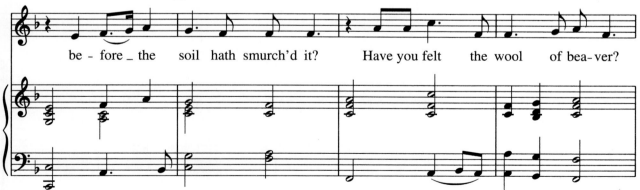

be - fore _ the soil hath smurch'd it? Have you felt the wool of bea-ver?

[1] The original poem has "white" in one version and "bright" in another;
either version may be chosen for performance.

HAVE YOU SEEN BUT A WHITE LILLIE GROW

MEDIUM LOW VOICE

Ben Jonson

Anonymous
ed. KEM

Have you seen but a white[1] lil - lie grow _____ be - fore rude hands had touch'd it; Have you mark'd _ but _ the _ fall of the snow be - fore _ the soil hath smurch'd it? Have you felt the wool of bea-ver?

[1] The original poem has "white" in one version and "bright" in another; either version may be chosen for performance.

BLOW, BLOW, THOU WINTER WIND

MEDIUM HIGH VOICE

William Shakespeare

Thomas A. Arne
(1710 - 1778)
ed. KEM

BLOW, BLOW, THOU WINTER WIND

MEDIUM LOW VOICE

William Shakespeare

Thomas A. Arne
(1710 - 1778)
ed. KEM

cause thou art not seen, ___ Al - tho' __ thy __ breath be
friend re - mem - ber'd not. ___ Thy sting __ is __ not so

cresc.

rude, al - tho' __ thy __ breath be rude, _____ al -
sharp as friend __ re - mem - ber'd not, _____ as ___

cresc.

f

tho' __ thy __ breath __ be rude.
friend __ re - mem - ber'd __ not.

D.S.

D.S.

f

ENGLISH SONGS

SHENANDOAH

MEDIUM HIGH VOICE

Sea Chanty
Arranged by Celius Dougherty

O Shen-an-do-ah, __ I hear you call-ing, Hi - o! you roll-ing riv-er, O Shen-an-do-ah, __ I long to hear you, Hi - o! I'm bound a-way

'Cross the wide Mis - sou - ri. Mis -
sou - ri she's — a might-y riv - er, Hi - o! you roll-ing
riv - er, When she rolls down — her top-sails shiv - er, Hi -

Shen-an-do-ah, _ I'll not de-ceive you, Hi - o! I'm bound a - way,

'Cross the wide Mis - sou - ri.

SHENANDOAH

MEDIUM LOW VOICE

Sea Chanty
Arranged by Celius Dougherty

O Shen-an-do-ah, __ I hear you call-ing, Hi - o! you roll-ing riv-er, O Shen-an-do-ah, __ I long to hear you, Hi - o! I'm bound a-way,

'Cross the wide Mis - sou - ri. Mis -
sou - ri she's ___ a might-y riv - er, Hi - o! you roll-ing
riv - er, When she rolls down ___ her top-sails shiv - er, Hi -

OH SLEEP, WHY DOST THOU LEAVE ME?

From *Semele*

MEDIUM HIGH VOICE

William Congreve

George F. Handel
(1685 - 1759)
Friederich Chrysander, ed.

Oh _____ sleep, oh _ sleep, oh sleep a-gain de-ceive me, oh

sleep, a-gain de-ceive me, to my arms re-store _ my _ wan - d'ring _ love, my wan -

d'ring love, re-store my wan-d'ring _ love! a-gain de-ceive me, oh _ sleep!

to my_ arms, to my _ arms re - store _____ my wan - d'ring

love!

OH SLEEP, WHY DOST THOU LEAVE ME?

From *Semele*

MEDIUM LOW VOICE

William Congreve

George F. Handel
(1685 - 1759)
Friederich Chrysander, ed.

Oh _____ sleep, oh _ sleep, why dost thou leave _ me? Why dost thou leave _ me? Why thy vi-sion-ar-yjoys re-move?

Oh _____ sleep, oh __ sleep, oh sleep a-gain de-ceive me, oh

15

sleep, a - gain de - ceive me, to my arms re-store _ my _ wan - d'ring _ love, my wan -

DOWN AMONG THE DEAD MEN

MEDIUM HIGH VOICE

Old English Air
ed. KEM

1. Here's health to the Queen and a lasting peace, To faction an end, to wealth increase; Come, let us drink it while we've breath, For there's no drinking
2. Let charming beauty's health go round, In whom celestial joys are found; And may confusion still pursue The senseless woman
3. In smiling Bacchus' joys I'll roll, Deny no pleasure to my soul; Let Bacchus' health round briskly move, For Bacchus is a
4. May love and wine their rites maintain, And their united pleasures reign, While Bacchus' treasure crowns the board, We'll sing the joys that

DOWN AMONG THE DEAD MEN

MEDIUM LOW VOICE

Old English Air
ed. KEM

DIDO'S LAMENT

From *Dido and Aeneas*

MEDIUM HIGH VOICE

Henry Purcell
(1659 - 1695)
ed. KEM

re - mem - ber me, But ah! _____ for - get my fate; Re-

mem - ber me, but ah! _____ for - get my _ fate!

DIDO'S LAMENT

From *Dido and Aeneas*

MEDIUM LOW VOICE

Henry Purcell
(1659 - 1695)
ed. KEM

trou - ble in ___ thy breast. Re - mem - ber me, re -

mem - ber me, But ah! ___ for - get my fate; Re -

mem - ber me, but ah! ___ for - get my _ fate; Re - mem - ber me,

re - mem - ber me, But ah! _____ for - get my fate; Re -

mem - ber me, but ah! _____ for - get my _ fate!

I ATTEMPT FROM LOVE'S SICKNESS TO FLY

From *The Indian Queen*

MEDIUM HIGH VOICE

Henry Purcell
(1659 - 1695)
ed. KEM

I at-tempt from love's

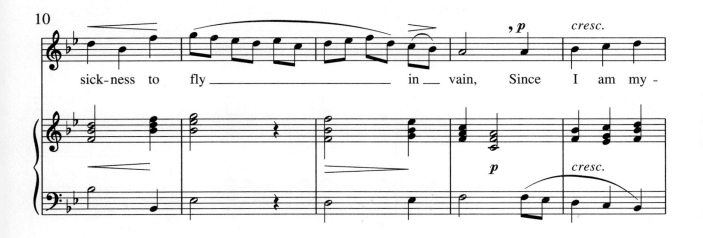

sick-ness to fly _____ in __ vain, Since I am my-

self   my own   fe - ver, Since   I   am   my - self   my own   fe - ver __ and __

pain,   No   more now,   no   more now,   fond __ heart,   with   pride   no more

swell,   Thou canst not __ raise __ for - ces, Thou   canst   not __ raise __ for - ces   e -

NOTE: The last twelve counts of the accompaniment may be repeated as an optional ending.
* Optional notes added.

I ATTEMPT FROM LOVE'S SICKNESS TO FLY

From *The Indian Queen*

MEDIUM LOW VOICE

Henry Purcell
(1659 - 1695)
ed. KEM

I at-tempt from love's

sick-ness to fly _____ in __ vain, Since I am my-

15

self my own fe - ver, Since I am my - self my own fe - ver __ and __

20

p *cresc.*

pain, No more now, no more now, fond __ heart, with pride no more

25

mf

swell, Thou canst not __ raise __ for - ces, Thou canst not __ raise __ for - ces e -

For Love has more pow'r, and less mer - cy than Fate, To make us ___ seek ___ ru - in, To ___

make ___ us ___ seek ___ ru - in, and ___ love those ___ that ___ hate. I at -

NOTE: The last twelve counts of the accompaniment may be repeated as an optional ending.

* Optional notes added.

O MISTRESS MINE

MEDIUM HIGH VOICE

William Shakespeare

Roger Quilter
(1877 - 1953)

Allegro moderato (♩ = 80)

O mis-tress mine, where are you roam-ing? O __ stay and hear, your true love's com - ing, That can sing both high and

kiss   me, Sweet-and-twen - ty,   Youth's a stuff   will   not en -

dure,   not   en - dure.____   Mis - tress

mine,   where   are   you   roam - ing?

O MISTRESS MINE

MEDIUM LOW VOICE

William Shakespeare

Roger Quilter
(1877 - 1953)

O mis-tress mine, where are you roam - ing? O stay and

hear, your true love's com - ing, That can sing both high and

What is love? 'tis not here - af - ter; Pre - sent mirth hath pre - sent laugh - ter; What's to come is still un - sure: In de - lay there lies no plen - ty; Then come

kiss   me, Sweet - and - twen - ty,   Youth's   a   stuff   will   not   en -

dure,   not   en -   dure. ____   Mis - tress

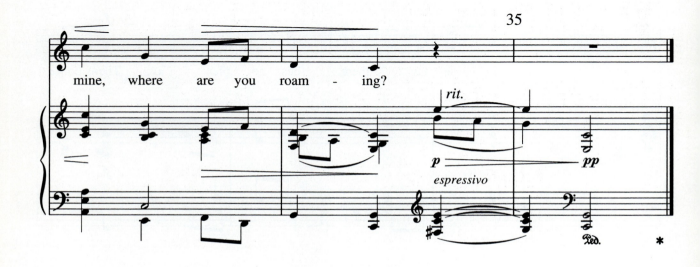

mine,   where   are   you   roam -   ing?

SIMPLE GIFTS

MEDIUM HIGH VOICE

Shaker Tune
ed. KEM

love and de-light. When true sim - plic - i - ty is gain'd, to bow and to bend we shan't be a-sham'd, To turn, turn will

be our de-light, Till by turn - ing, turn - ing we come 'round right.

NOTE: The last eight counts of the accompaniment may be repeated as an optional ending.

SIMPLE GIFTS

MEDIUM LOW VOICE

Shaker Tune
ed. KEM

'Tis the gift to be sim-ple, 'tis the gift to be free, 'Tis the gift to come down where we ought to be, And when we find our-selves in the place just right, 'Twill be in the val-ley of

NOTE: The last eight counts of the accompaniment may be repeated as an optional ending.

PRETTY RING TIME

MEDIUM HIGH VOICE

William Shakespeare

Peter Warlock
(1894 - 1930)

ENGLISH SONGS

life was but a flow'r In the spring time, the

on - ly pret - ty ring time, When birds do sing Hey ding a ding ding, Sweet

lov - ers love the spring.   And there - fore take the pres - ent

time, With a hey and a ho and a hey no - ni - no, For love is

crown - èd with the prime In the spring time, the on - ly pret-ty ring time, When

birds do sing Hey ding a ding ding, Sweet lov - ers love the spring.

PRETTY RING TIME

MEDIUM LOW VOICE

William Shakespeare

Peter Warlock
(1894 - 1930)

life was but a flow'r In the spring time, the on-ly pret-ty ring time, When birds do sing Hey ding a ding ding, Sweet lov-ers love the spring. And there-fore take the pres-ent

pp staccatissimo sempre

SEBBEN, CRUDELE

Savage and Heartless

MEDIUM HIGH VOICE

Translation by
James P. Dunn*

Antonio Caldara
(1670 - 1736)
ed. KEM

Seb - ben, cru - de - le, mi fai lan - guir, ___ sem - pre fe -
Sav - age and heart - less is your cruel scorn, ___ Faith - ful and

de - le, sem - pre fe - de - le ti vo - glio a - mar.
daunt - less, Faith - ful and daunt - less is my love in turn.

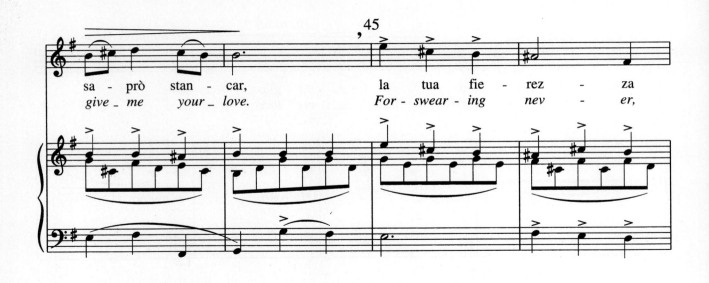

sa - prò stan - car,　　　la　tua　fie - rez - za
give _ me　your _ love.　　　For - swear - ing　nev - er,

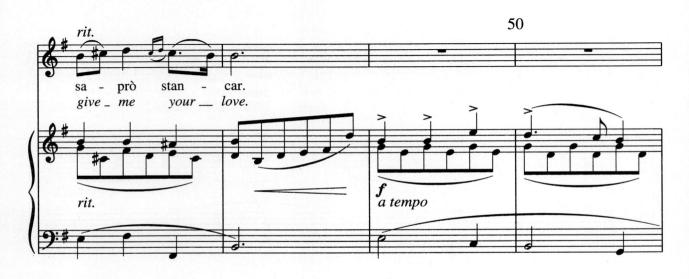

sa - prò stan - car.
give _ me　your _ love.

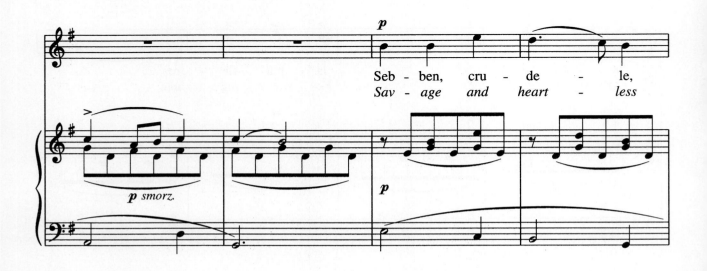

Seb - ben,　cru - de - le,
Sav - age　and　heart - less

sem - pre_ fe - de - le ti_ vo - glio a - mar,
Faith - ful_ and_ daunt - less is_ my love in turn.

seb - ben, cru - de - le, mi fai lan - guir,_____
Sav - age and heart - less is your cruel scorn,_____

sem - pre_ fe - de - le ti_ vo - glio a - mar._____
Faith - ful_ and_ daunt - less is_ my love in_ turn._____

SEBBEN, CRUDELE

Savage and Heartless

MEDIUM LOW VOICE

Translation by
James P. Dunn*

Antonio Caldara
(1670 - 1736)
ed. KEM

Seb - ben, cru - de - le, mi fai lan - guir,_____
Sav - age and heart - less is your cruel scorn,_____

sem - pre__ fe - de - le ti__ vo - glio a - mar.
Faith - ful__ and__ daunt - less is__ my love in turn.

Seb - ben, cru - de - le, mi fai lan - guir,_____
Sav - age and heart - less is your cruel scorn,_____

sa - prò stan - car,
give _ me your _ love.

la tua fie - rez - za
For - swear - ing nev - er,

sa - prò stan - car.
give _ me your _ love.

Seb - ben, cru - de - le,
Sav - age and heart - less

VITTORIA, MIO CORE!

Victorious, my heart is!

MEDIUM HIGH VOICE

Adap. from English
text by H. Millard

Giacomo Carissimi
(1605 - 1674)
ed. KEM

Allegro con brio

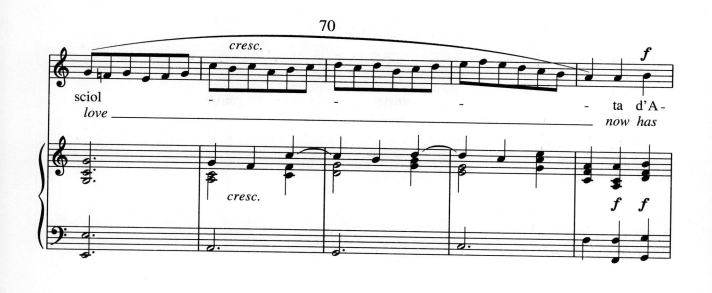

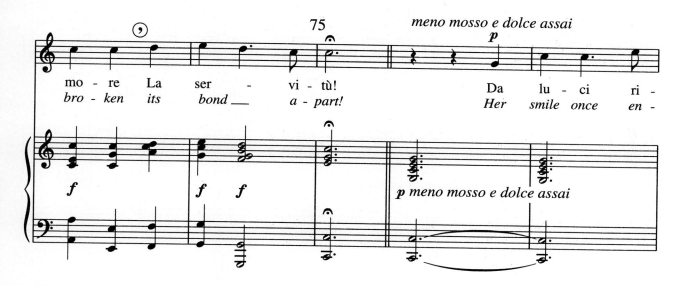

ven - - ti: Nel duol, ne' tor - men - ti lo più non mi sfac -
heal - - ing; All sor - row and tor-ment no long - er I'm fear -

cio È rot - to o - gni lac - cio, Spa - ri - to il ti - mo -
ing, Now bro - ken each tie is, all fears dis - ap - pear -

Tempo I

re! Vit - to - ria! Vit - to - ria! Vit - to - ria! Vit - to - ria, mio co -
ing! Vic - to - rious, Vic - to - rious, Vic - to - rious, Vic - to - rious, my heart

VITTORIA, MIO CORE!

Victorious, my heart is!

MEDIUM LOW VOICE

Adap. from English
text by H. Millard

Giacomo Carissimi
(1605 - 1674)
ed. KEM

co - re! Non la - gri - mar più, È sciol - ta __ d'A -
heart __ is! And tears are in vain, For love now __ has __

mo - re __ La __ vil ser - vi - tù, È sciol - - -
bro - ken __ its __ bond __ a - part; For love _____

- - ta d'A - mo - re La ser - vi - tù.
now has bro - ken its bond __ a - part.

ven - ti: Nel duol, ne' tor - men - ti lo più non mi sfac -
heal - ing; All sor - row and tor - ment no long - er I'm fear -

cio È rot - to o - gni lac - cio, Spa - ri - to il ti - mo -
ing, Now bro - ken each tie is, all fears dis - ap - pear -

Tempo I

re! Vit - to - ria! Vit - to - ria! Vit - to - ria! Vit - to - ria, mio co -
ing! Vic - to - rious, Vic - to - rious, Vic - to - rious, Vic - to - rious, my heart __

VERGIN, TUTTO AMOR

Virgin, full of love

MEDIUM HIGH VOICE

Translation by
James P. Dunn*

Francesco Durante
(1684 - 1755)
ed. KEM

Largo religioso

ff

rit.

5

pp

Ver - gin, tut - to a - mor, o ma - dre di bon -
Vir - gin, full of love, O queen of grace and

pp a tempo

simile

ta - de, o ma - dre pi - a, ma - dre pi - a, a-scol - ta, dol-ce Ma-
mer - cy, O Bless-ed Moth - er, pure and ho - ly, O hear my pray - er,

ri - a, la____ vo - ce del pec-ca-tor,____ del____ pec - ca -
gen - tle Mar-y, O hear the voice_ of this____ sin - ner, of this

tor.
sin - ner.

Il pian - to suo ti
O may his weep - ing

muo - va, giun - ga - no a te __ i suoi la - men - tí, suo duol, suoi tri - sti ac-
move you, And may you heed _ his lam - en - ta - tions, His grief, his sad mourn-ful

15

cen - ti, sen - ti pie - to - so quel _ tuo cor, _ pie-to - so, pie-to-
cry - ing, Be there com-pas - sion in _ your heart _ O queen _____ of grace ___

p

cresc. assai

so, pie - to - so quel _ tuo cor, quel tuo
_____ and mer - cy, in _ your heart, in your

cor. O ma-dre di bon-ta-de Ver-gin, tut-to a-mor, o ma-dre di bon-
heart. O Vir-gin, full of love,__ Vir-gin, full of love, O Vir-gin, full of

ta-de, o Ver-gin, tut-to a-mo-re, Ver-gin, tut-to a-mor,__
*love,*__ O Vir-gin, full__ of love,__ O Vir-gin, full__ of love,__

Ver-gin, tut-to a-mor.
Vir-gin, full of__ love.

poco rit.

VERGIN, TUTTO AMOR

Virgin, full of love

MEDIUM LOW VOICE

Translation by
James P. Dunn*

Francesco Durante
(1684 - 1755)
ed. KEM

cor.
heart.

O ma-dre di_bon-ta-de Ver-gin, tut-to a-mor, o ma-dre di_bon-
O Vir-gin, full_of love,_ Vir-gin, full of love, O Vir-gin, full_of

ta - de, o Ver-gin, tut-to a-mo-re, Ver-gin, tut-to a-mor, _____
love, _____ O Vir-gin, full_of love,_ O Vir-gin, full_of love, _____

_____ Ver-gin, tut-to a-mor.
_____ *Vir-gin, full of _____ love.*

poco rit.

O DEL MIO DOLCE ARDOR

O thou belov'd
(From *Paride ed Elena*)

MEDIUM HIGH VOICE

Translation by
James P. Dunn*

Cristoforo Gluck
(1714 - 1787)
ed. KEM

Moderato (♩ = 46)

p dolcissimo

O del mio dol - ce ar -
O thou my own true

dor _____ bra - ma - to og - get -
love, _____ O thou my long -

to, bra - ma - to og - get - to,
ing, De - sire and long - ing,

L'au - ra che tu re - spi - ri,
Dear - est, at last I'm near _____ you,

10

al - fin re - spi - ro,
How I a - dore _____ you!

al - fin _____ re -
How I _____ a -

m'em - pie il pet - to Cer - co te,
swel - ling with - in___ me, *You I seek,*

chia - mo te, spe -
you I call, *hop -*

ro e so spi - ro. Ah!___
ing and as - pi - ring. *Ah!___*

O DEL MIO DOLCE ARDOR

O thou belov'd
(From *Paride ed Elena*)

MEDIUM LOW VOICE

Translation by
James P. Dunn*

Cristoforo Gluck
(1714 - 1787)
ed. KEM

L'au - ra che tu re - spi - ri,
Dear - est, at last I'm near _____ you,

al - fin re - spi - ro,
How I a - dore _____ you!

al - fin _____ re -
How I _____ a -

mio pen - sier si fin - ge
ev - 'ry thought en-fold ____ you,

Le più lie
Hope and pas

cresc.

cresc.

te spe - ran
sion en - flames ____

dim. assai

ze;
me;

E nel de - si - o che co - si ____
And with these long - ings and de - sires ____

AH! MIO COR

Ah! My Heart (From *Alcina*)

MEDIUM HIGH VOICE

Translation by
James P. Dunn*

George F. Handel
(1685 - 1759)
ed. KEM

De - i, Nu - me d'a - mo - re! tra - di - to - re,
hear me! Venus! A - mo - re! False tor-men - ter,

t'a - mo tan - to, puoi la - sciar mi so - la in pian - to? Oh
how I love _ you, Can you leave me 'lone tor-ment - ed, Oh,

De - i! puoi la - sciar - mi, oh De - i, per - chè?
heav-ens! Can you leave _ me? Heav-ens! But why?

Ah! mio co - re, scher - ni - to se - i. __
Ah! my heart, __ de - spised and scorned. __

Stel - le, De - i, Nu - me d'a - mo - re! tra - di -
Heav - ens! Hear __ me! Ve - nus! A - mo - re! False tor -

to - re, t'a - mo tan - to, puoi la - sciar mi so - la in pian - to, oh
men - ter, how I love __ you. Can you leave me 'lone la - ment - ing? Oh,

puoi la-sciar-mi so-la in pian-to, oh De-i! puoi la-sciar-mi, oh De-i, per-
Can you leave me 'lone la-ment-ing, Oh, heav-ens! Can you leave me, oh, heav-ens, but

chè?
why?

AH! MIO COR

Ah! My Heart (From *Alcina*)

MEDIUM LOW VOICE

Translation by
James P. Dunn*

George F. Handel
(1685 - 1759)
ed. KEM

De - i, Nu - me d'a - mo - re! tra - di - to - re,
hear me! *Ve - nus!* *A - mo - re!* *False tor-men - ter,*

t'a - mo tan - to, puoi la - sciar mi - so - la in pian - to? Oh
how I love_ you, *Can you leave me 'lone tor-ment-ed,* *Oh,*

De - i! puoi la - sciar - mi, oh De - i, per - chè?
heav-ens! *Can you leave_ me? Heav-ens! But why?*

Ah! mio co - re, scher - ni - to se - i. __
Ah! my heart, __ de - spised and scorned. __

Stel - le, De - i, Nu - me d'a - mo - re! tra - di -
Heav - ens! Hear __ me! Ve - nus! A - mo - re! False tor -

to - re, t'a - mo tan - to, puoi la - sciar mi - so - la in pian - to, oh
men - ter, how I love __ you. Can you leave me 'lone la - ment - ing? Oh,

De — i,   puo — i la-sciar - mi   so - la,
heav - *ens!*   *Can* ___ *you* _ *leave* _ *me,*   *lone* - *ly,*

so - la,   so - la ___ in pian - to,   puoi la - sciar - mi,   oh
lone - *ly,*   *lone* - *ly, la* — *ment* - *ing,*   *Can* *you* *leave* *me,*   *oh,*

De — i,   per - chè?   per - chè?   per - chè?
heav - *ens*   *but why?*   *But* *why?*   *But* *why?*

puoi la - sciar - mi so - la in pian - to, oh De - i! puoi la - sciar - mi, oh De - i, per-
Can you leave me 'lone la-ment-ing, Oh, heav-ens! Can you leave me, oh, heav-ens, but

chè?
why?

OMBRA MAI FÙ

From *Serse*

MEDIUM HIGH VOICE

Verse by
Nicolò Minato

George F. Handel
(1685 - 1759)
ed. KEM

Ombra mai fù di vegetabile, cara ed amabile, soave più.
There never was a tree's shade that was more dear, charming, and sweet.

ma-bi-le, om - bra mai __ fù, di ve-ge-ta - bi-le ca-ra ed a-

ma - bi-le so - a - ve più, so - a - ve più.

OMBRA MAI FÙ

From *Serse*

MEDIUM LOW VOICE

Verse by
Nicolò Minato

George F. Handel
(1685 - 1759)
ed. KEM

Ombra mai fù di vegetabile, cara ed amabile, soave più.
There never was a tree's shade that was more dear, charming, and sweet.

ma - bi-le, om - bra mai _ fù, di ve-ge-ta - bi-le ca - ra ed a-

ma - bi-le so - a - ve più, so - a - ve più.

LASCIATEMI MORIRE

Let Me Die (From *Arianna*)

MEDIUM HIGH VOICE

Claudio Monteverdi
(1567 - 1643)
ed. KEM

Lasciatemi morire, E che volete
voi che mi conforte in cosi dura sorte,
in cosi gran martire?
Lasciatemi morire!

*Let me die! What can console me
in so hard a fate,
in such great torment?
Let me die!*

le - te _____ che mi con - for - te in co - si du - ra

sor - te, in co - si gran mar - ti - re? La - scia - te -

mi mo - ri - re, La - scia - te - mi mo - ri - re!

LASCIATEMI MORIRE

Let Me Die (From *Arianna*)

MEDIUM LOW VOICE

Claudio Monteverdi
(1567 - 1643)
ed. KEM

Lasciatemi morire, E che volete
voi che mi conforte in cosi dura sorte,
in cosi gran martire?
Lasciatemi morire!

Let me die! What can console me
in so hard a fate,
in such great torment?
Let me die!

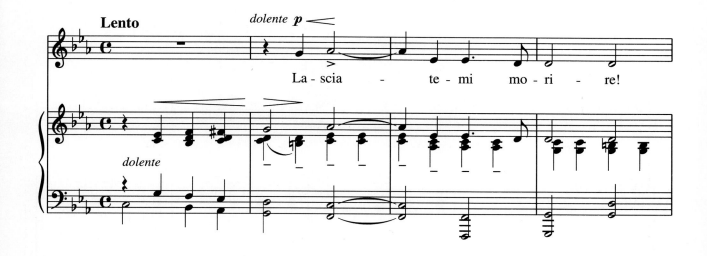

le - te _____ che mi con - for - te   in co - si du - ra

sor - te,   in co - si gran   mar - ti - re?   La - scia - te -

mi mo - ri - re,   La - scia - te - mi   mo - ri - re!

SE TU M'AMI

If Thou Lov'st Me

MEDIUM HIGH VOICE

Adap. from English
text by Theo. Baker

Attributed to
Giovanni Battista Pergolesi
(1710 - 1736)
ed. KEM

Ma se pen-si che so-let-to Io ti deb-ba ri - a-mar,
But if thou think tho' that de-mure-ly I on thee a-lone may smile,

Pa-sto-rel-lo, sei sog-get-to Fa-cil-men-te a t'in-gan nar;
Sim-ple shep-herd, thou art sure-ly Prone thy sen-ses to be-guile;

Pa-sto-rel-lo, sei sog-get-to Fa-cil-men-te a t'in-gan-nar.
Sim-ple shep-herd, thou art sure-ly Prone thy sen-ses to be-guile,

Ma de - gli uo mî - ni il ___ con - si - glio Io per me non se - gui - rò.
all men speak of maid - en - fol - ly Finds no fa - vor in mine eyes,

Non per - chè mi pia - ce il gi - glio Gli al-tri fio - ri sprez - ze - rò.
Nor be - cause I like the lil - y Shall I oth - er flow'rs de - spise.

Se tu __ m'a — mi, __ se tu so — spi — ri Sol __ per
If thou __ lov'st me, __ and sigh — est ev — er But __ for

me, __ gen — til __ pa — stor. Ho do — lor de' tuoi mar — ti — ri,
me, __ O gen — tle __ swain, Sweet I find thy lov — ing fa — vor,

Ho di — let — to del tuo a — mor, __ Ma se pen — si che so — let — to
Pit — i — ful I feel thy pain. __ Should'st __ thou __ think tho' that __ de — mure — ly

SE TU M'AMI

If Thou Lov'st Me

MEDIUM LOW VOICE

Adap. from English
text by Theo. Baker

Attributed to
Giovanni Battista Pergolesi
(1710 - 1736)
ed. KEM

Se tu ___ m'a - mi, ___ se tu so - spi - ri Sol _ per me, gen - til pa -
If thou ___ lov'st me, ___ and sigh - est ev - er But _ for me, O gen - tle ___

stor, Ho do - lor de' tuoi mar - ti - ri, Ho di - let - to del tuo _ a - mor, ___
swain, Sweet I find thy lov - ing fa - vor, Pit - i - ful I feel thy pain. ___

Ma _ se _ pen - si che _ so - let - to Io _ ti deb - ba ri - a - mar,
But if thou _ think tho' that _ de - mure - ly I _ on _ thee a - lone _ may smile,

Pa - sto - rel - lo, sei sog - get - to Fa - cil - men - te a t'in - gan nar;
Sim - ple shep - herd, thou art sure - ly Prone thy _ sen - ses to be - guile;

Pa - sto - rel - lo, sei sog - get - to Fa - cil - men - te a t'in - gan - nar.
Sim - ple shep - herd, thou art sure - ly Prone _ thy _ sen - ses _ to be - guile,

Ma de-gli uo mî-ni il ___ con-si-glio Io per me non se-gui-rò.
all men speak of maid - en-fol - ly Finds no fa - vor in mine eyes,

Non per-chè mi pia-ce il gi-glio Gli al-tri fio-ri sprez-ze-rò.
Nor be-cause I like the lil - y Shall I oth-er flow'rs de-spise.

SE FLORINDO È FEDELE

If Florindo Be Constant

MEDIUM HIGH VOICE

Translation by
James P. Dunn*

Alessandro Scarlatti
(1659 - 1725)
ed. KEM

SE FLORINDO È FEDELE

If Florindo Be Constant

MEDIUM LOW VOICE

Translation by
James P. Dunn*

Alessandro Scarlatti
(1659 - 1725)
ed. KEM

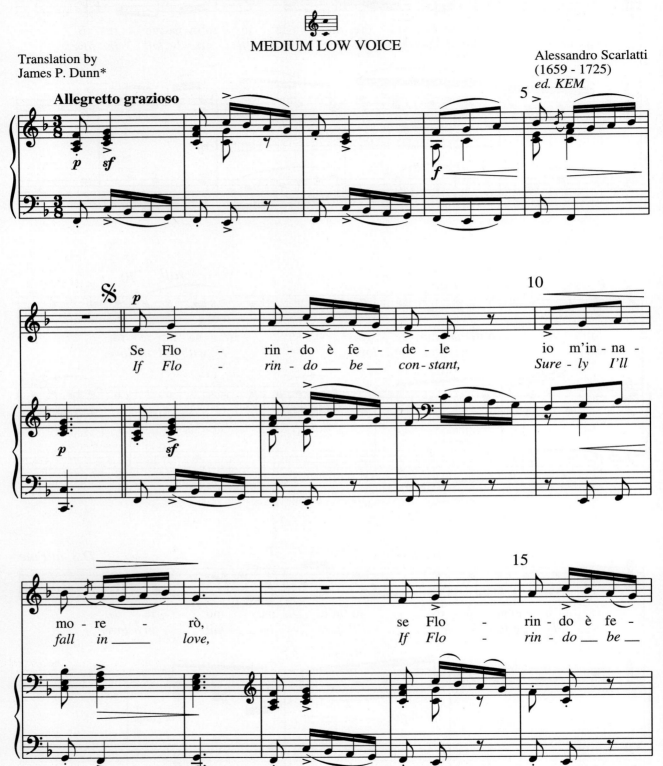

Se Flo - rin - do è fe - de - le io m'in - na -
If Flo - rin - do __ be __ con - stant, Sure - ly I'll

mo - re - rò, se Flo - rin - do è fe -
fall in ____ love, If Flo - rin - do __ be __

de - le   io m'in - na - mo - re - rò,   s'è __ fe - de - le __ Flo -
con - stant,   Sure - ly I'll   fall in _____ love,   If __ Flo - rin - do __ be

rin - do min - na - mo - re - rò,   io m'in - na - mo - re -
con - stant, I ____ will _ fall in   love,   Sure - ly I'll   fall   in _____

rò,   sè __ fe - de - le __ Flo - rin - do m'in - na - mo - re - rò,
love, If __ Flo - rin - do __ be   con - stant I ____ will __ fall   in   love,

cier,
guile.
ch'io mi-sa-prò di—fen—de-re d'un guar — do
No   doubt I can re-sist,   I know, the sweet—est

lu - sin - ghier.
wink — or — smile.
Pre - ghi   pian - ti
Moan - ing,   sigh-ing,

e que-re-le, io non-a-scol-te-rò
weep - ing, cry-ing, my heart will ne - ver cleave.
ma se sa - rà fe-
But if she should be

de - le, ma se sa - rà fe - de - le io m'in-na-mo - re - rò,
con - stant. *But if she should be con - stant, I'll sure-ly fall in love,*

p   *dolce*   *rall.* 70

io m'in-na - mo - re - rò, m'in-na-mo-re - rò,
yes, *I will fall in love.* *I will fall in love.*

a tempo   *p*   D.S. al Fine

m'in-na - mo - re - rò, io m'in - na - mo - re - rò.
I will fall in love, *I'll sure - ly ___ fall in love.*

a tempo ___   *col canto*

D.S. al Fine

TU LO SAI

You Know Quite Well

MEDIUM HIGH VOICE

Giuseppe Torelli
(1658 - 1709)
ed. KEM

NOTE: The four-measure introduction is optional.

TU LO SAI

You Know Quite Well

MEDIUM LOW VOICE

Giuseppe Torelli
(1658 - 1709)
ed. KEM

Andantino

Tu lo _____ sai quan-to t'a - ma - i, Tu lo _____
You know _ quite well how much I love you. You know _ quite

sai, lo sai cru- del! ___ Io non bra - mo
well O heart-less ___ one. ___ No - thing more ___

NOTE: The four-measure introduction is optional.

ICH LIEBE DICH SO WIE DU MICH

I Love Thee

MEDIUM HIGH VOICE

Carl Friedrich Wilhelm Herrosee

Ludwig van Beethoven
(1770 - 1827)
ed. KEM

Ich lie - be dich so wie du mich, Am A - bend und am
I love thee as thou lov - est me, At eve - ning or at

Mor - gen, Noch war kein Tag, wo du und ich Nicht
morn - ing, For not a day goes by but we have

teil - ten uns - re Sor - gen.
shared each oth - er's sor - row,
Auch
Our

waren sie für dich und mich Ge- teilt leicht zu er-
cares ___ *all the light* - *er seem'd Be* - *cause we al* - *ways* ___

tra - gen; Du trö- ste- test im Kum- mer mich, Ich ___
shar'd ___ *them; When I was sad, you cheered* ___ *me and* ___

weint' in dei- ne Kla- gen, in dei- ne
all thy cares I shar'd them, thy cares I

ICH LIEBE DICH SO WIE DU MICH

I Love Thee

MEDIUM LOW VOICE

Carl Friedrich Wilhelm Herrosee

Ludwig van Beethoven
(1770 - 1827)
ed. KEM

waren sie für dich und mich Ge - teilt leicht zu - er -
cares___ all the light - er seem'd Be - cause we al - ways___

tra - gen; Du trö - ste - test im Kum - mer mich, Ich___
shar'd___ them; When I was sad, you cheered___ me and___

weint' in dei - ne Kla - gen, in dei - ne
all thy cares I shar'd them, thy cares I

20

Kla - gen. Drum Got - tes Se - gen ü - ber dir, Du mei - nes Le - bens
shar'd them. Then grace of heav'n in all my life, God's own bless-ing

25

Freu - de, Gott schüt - ze dich, er - halt' dich mir, Schütz'
rest on thee. May God guard thee oh my be-lov'd, and

und er - halt' uns bei - de, Gott schüt - ze dich, er -
bless thee past all mea - sure! May God guard thee, oh

STILL WIE DIE NACHT

Still as the Night

MEDIUM HIGH VOICE

Carl Bohm
(1844 - 1920)
ed. KEM

Still wie die Nacht, tief wie das Meer,
Still as the night, deep as the sea,

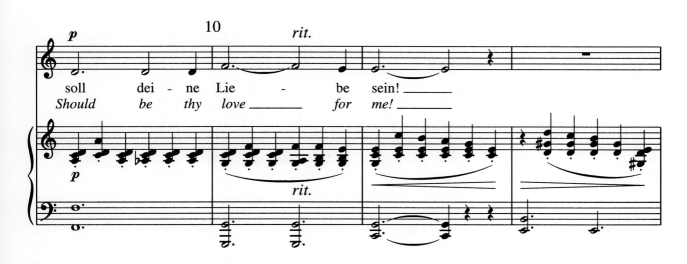

soll dei - ne Lie - be sein!
Should be thy love for me!

Still wie die Nacht, _____ und tief wie das Meer
Still as the night, _____ and deep as the sea,

soll dei - ne Lie - be, dei - ne Lie - be sein, _____
Thy love should be, thy love should be _____ for me. _____

soll dei - ne Lie - be sein!
Thy love should be _____ for me!

Wenn du mich liebst so wie ich dich,
Lov - est thou me as I love thee,

will ich dein ei - gen sein.
I am for-ev - er thine.

Heiss wie der Stahl, und fest wie der Stein
Glow - ing as steel, and strong as a stone.

soll dei - ne Lie - be, dei - ne Lie - be sein,_____
Thy love should be, thy love should be _____ my own,_____

soll dei - ne Lie - be sein! _____
Thy love should be _____ my own. _____

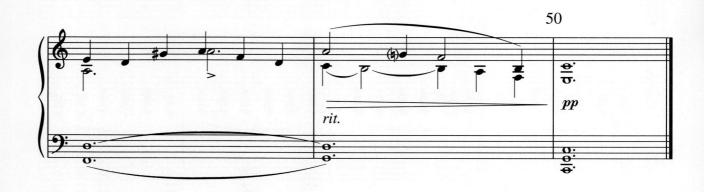

STILL WIE DIE NACHT

Still as the Night

MEDIUM LOW VOICE

Carl Bohm
(1844 - 1920)
ed. KEM

Still wie die Nacht, tief wie das Meer,
Still as the night, deep as the sea,

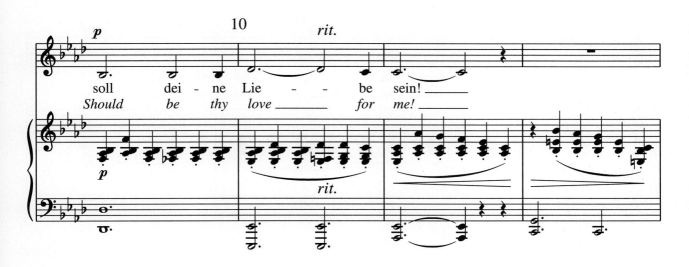

soll dei - ne Lie - be sein!
Should be thy love for me!

Wenn du mich liebst so wie ich dich,
Lov - est thou me as I love thee,

will ich dein ei - gen sein.
I am for - ev - er thine.

Heiss ___ wie der Stahl, ___ und fest wie der Stein
Glow - ing as steel, ___ and strong as a stone.

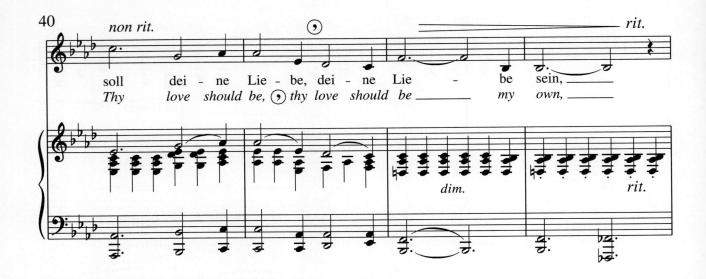

soll dei - ne Lie - be, dei - ne Lie - be sein, _____
Thy love should be, thy love should be _____ my own, _____

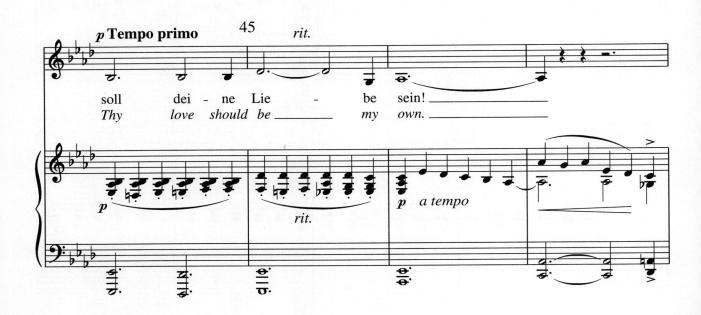

soll dei - ne Lie - be sein! _____
Thy love should be _____ my own. _____

SAPPHISCHE ODE

Sapphic Ode

MEDIUM HIGH VOICE

Hans Schmidt

Johannes Brahms
(1833 - 1897)
ed. KEM

Ro - sen brach ich nachts mir am dunk - len
Ros - es I at night cull from dark - 'ning

Ha - ge; Süs - ser hauch - ten Duft sie, als je _____ am
hedge - rows, Breathe a sweet - er fra - grance than day _____ dis -

Ta - ge; Doch ver - streu - ten reich die be - weg - ten
clos - es, And the trem - bling pet - als when I _____ dis -

15

SAPPHISCHE ODE

Sapphic Ode

MEDIUM LOW VOICE

Hans Schmidt

Johannes Brahms
(1833 - 1897)
ed. KEM

Ro - sen brach ich nachts mir am dunk - len
Ros - es I at night cull from dark - 'ning

Ha - ge; Süs - ser hauch - ten Duft sie, als je _____ am
hedge - rows, Breathe a sweet - er fra - grance than day _____ dis-

Ta - ge; Doch ver - streu - ten reich die be - weg - ten
clos - es, And the trem - bling pet - als when I _____ dis-

rück - te,
charmed ___ me.
Die ich nachts vom Strauch dei - ner Lip - pen
Kiss - es I at night from thy lips ___ have

pflück - te:
tak - en,
Doch auch dir, be - wegt im Ge - müt ___ gleich
and so moved wert thou when my kiss - es

je - nen,
wooed thee,
Tau - ten die Trä -
that tear - drops be - dew'd ___

nen.
me.

GUTE NACHT

Good Night

MEDIUM HIGH VOICE

Joseph von Eichendorff

Robert Franz
(1815 - 1892)
ed. KEM

sollt', _____ ob es Lieb - chen grüs - sen soll't? O
not, _____ May I greet my love or not? O

Vög - lein, du hast dich be - tro - gen, sie woh - net nicht mehr im
bird, thy fate I'm _____ la - ment - ing, No more doth she sing in the

Tal, _____ schwing' auf dich zum Him - mel's bo - gen, gruss' sie
vale, _____ Wing forth to the heav'n a - bove _____ thee, Greet her

dro - ben zum letz - ten - mal. _____
there with my last fare - well. _____

GUTE NACHT

Good Night

MEDIUM LOW VOICE

Joseph von Eichendorff

Robert Franz
(1815 - 1892)
ed. KEM

Die Höh'n und Wäld - er schon
The hills and for - ests are

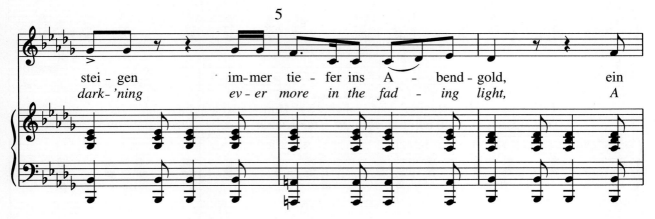

stei - gen im-mer tie - fer ins A - bend-gold, ein
dark-'ning ev - er more in the fad - ing light, A

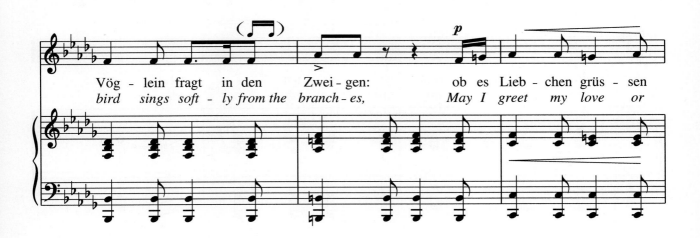

Vög - lein fragt in den Zwei - gen: ob es Lieb - chen grüs - sen
bird sings soft - ly from the branch - es, May I greet my love or

UNGEDULD

Impatience
From *Die Schöne Müllerin*

MEDIUM HIGH VOICE

Wilhelm Muller
Translation by
Frederic Kirchberger*

Franz Schubert
(1797 - 1828)
ed. KEM

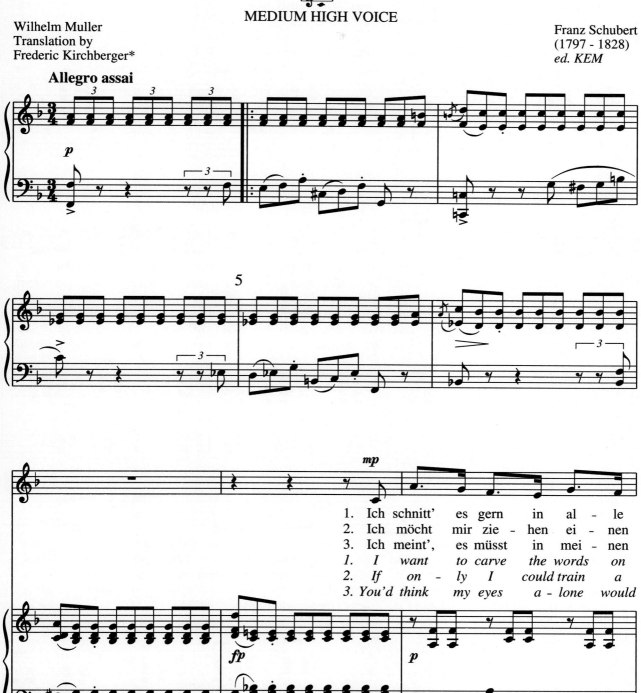

UNGEDULD

Impatience

From *Die Schöne Müllerin*

MEDIUM LOW VOICE

Wilhelm Muller
Translation by
Frederic Kirchberger*

Franz Schubert
(1797 - 1828)
ed. KEM

Allegro assai

5

1. Ich schnitt' es gern in al - le
2. Ich möcht mir zie - hen ei - nen
3. Ich meint', es müsst in mei - nen

1. *I want to carve the words on*
2. *If on - ly I could train a*
3. *You'd think my eyes a - lone would*

DU BIST WIE EINE BLUME

Thou Art Just Like a Flower

MEDIUM HIGH VOICE

Heinrich Heine

Robert Schumann
(1810 - 1856)
ed. KEM

ist, _____ als ob ich die Hän - de auf's Haupt dir le - gen
hands _____ in lov-ing de - vo - tion, I'd rest up - on _____ thy

sollt', be - tend, das Gott dich er - hal - te
brow, Pray - ing that God may e'er keep thee

so rein und schön und hold.
As love - ly, pure, and fair.

DU BIST WIE EINE BLUME

Thou Art Just Like a Flower

MEDIUM LOW VOICE

Heinrich Heine

Robert Schumann
(1810 - 1856)
ed. KEM

ist, _____ als ob ich die Hän – de auf's Haupt dir le – gen

hands _____ in lov-ing de – vo – tion, I'd rest up-on _____ thy

sollt', be – tend, das Gott dich er – hal – te

brow, Pray – ing that God may e'er keep thee

so rein und schön und hold.

As love – ly, pure, and fair.

ICH GROLLE NICHT

I'll Not Complain

MEDIUM HIGH VOICE

Heinrich Heine

Robert Schumann
(1810 - 1856)
ed. KEM

nicht, ich grol - le nicht. Wie du auch
plain, I'll not com-plain. How-e'er thou

strahlst in Di - a - man - ten-pracht, es fällt kein Strahl in dei - nes
shin'st in dia-mond splen-dor bright. There falls no ray in-to thy

Herz - ens Nacht; das weiss ich längst.
heart's deep night, I know full well.

Ich grol - le nicht und wenn das Herz _____ auch
I'll not com-plain, tho' break my heart _____ in

bricht. Ich sah dich ja im Trau - me und sah die
twain. In dreams I saw thee wan - ing, and saw the

Nacht in dei-nes Her - zens Rau - me, und sah die Schlang' die' dir am Her - zen
night with-in thy bo - som reign-ing, And saw the snake that on thy heart doth

*Indicated as optional by composer.

ICH GROLLE NICHT

I'll Not Complain

MEDIUM LOW VOICE

Heinrich Heine

Robert Schumann
(1810 - 1856)
ed. KEM

*Indicated as optional by composer.

ALLERSEELEN

All Souls' Day

MEDIUM HIGH VOICE

Hermann von Gilm

Richard Strauss
(1864 - 1849)
ed. KEM

Tranquillo

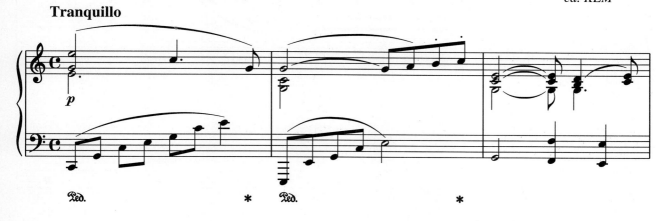

Stell' auf den Tisch die duf-ten-den Re - se - den, die
Place on the ta - ble sweet mi-gnon-ettes be - fore us, The

ALLERSEELEN

All Souls' Day

MEDIUM LOW VOICE

Hermann von Gilm

Richard Strauss
(1864 - 1849)
ed. KEM

Stell' auf den Tisch die duf-ten-den Re-se - den, die
Place on the ta-ble sweet mi-gnon-ettes be-fore us, The

letz - ten ro - ten A - stern trag' her - bei,
last red as - ters bring be-fore they de - cay,
und lass uns
And let us

wie - der von der Lie - be re - den, wie einst im
speak a - gain of love to - geth - er, As once in

Mai._____
May._____

Gib mir die Hand, dass ich sie heim-lich drü-cke, und wenn man's sieht,
Give me your hand a - gain in sweet sur-ren - der, It mat - ters not

_ mir ist es ei - ner - lei, gib mir nur ei - nen dei - ner süs - sen
_ what an - y one may say; Give _ me one glance, warm and sweet and

Bli - cke, wie einst im Mai.
ten - der, As once in May.

BEAU SOIR

Evening Fair

MEDIUM HIGH VOICE

Paul Bourget

Claude Debussy
(1862 - 1918)
ed. KEM

son court sur les champs de blé,_____
glow spreads o'er the fields of grain,_____

Un con - seil d'être heu - reux sem - ble sor - tir des
Comes a call to be glad, that seems from all things

cho - ses Et mon - ter vers le
stream - ing Doth a - rise toward my

beau, _____

fair, _____

Car nous nous en al – lons,

For we shall all de – part,

com – me s'en va cette on – de

as shin – ing wa – ters flow – ing

BEAU SOIR

Evening Fair

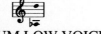

MEDIUM LOW VOICE

Paul Bourget

Claude Debussy
(1862 - 1918)
ed. KEM

FRENCH SONGS

son court sur les champs de blé, _____
glow spreads o'er the fields of grain, _____

Un con - seil d'être heu - reux sem - ble sor - tir des
Comes a call to be glad, that seems from all things

cho - ses Et mon - ter vers le
stream - ing Doth a - rise toward my

beau, _____
fair, _____

Car nous nous en al - lons,
For we shall all de - part,

com - me s'en va cette on - de
as shin - ing wa - ters flow - ing

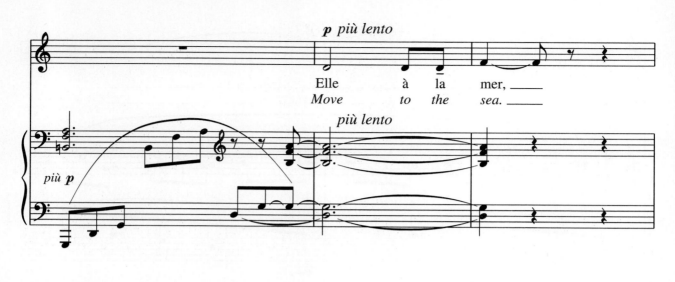

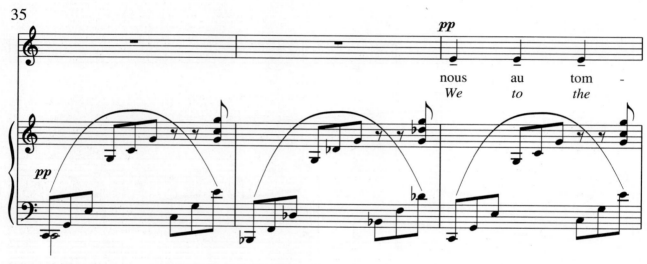

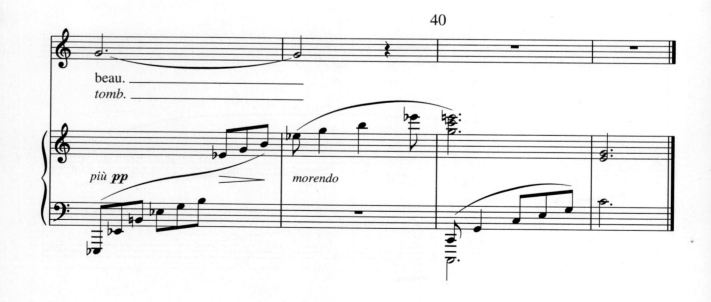

ROMANCE

MEDIUM HIGH VOICE

Paul Bourget

Claude Debussy
(1862 - 1918)
ed. KEM

L'âme é - va - po - rée et souf-
The soul _ of fleet - ing and

fran - te, L'â - me dou - ce, l'âme o - do - ran - te Des lis di - vins _
suff - ering, Soul so gen - tle, O fra-grant scent _ of li - ly fair, _

_ que j'ai cueil - li Dans le jar - din de ta pen - sée,
_ that I have gath - ered in the gar - den of your _ thought,

Où donc les vents l'ont-ils chas - sée,
Oh, where __ is it borne a - way,
Cette âme a - do - ra - ble des
This soul, oh so pure and so

lis?
fair?

meno mosso
pp

N'est - il plus un par - fum qui res - te
Is no per - fume __ still re - main - ing

De la su - a - vi - té cé - les - te Des jours où tu m'en - ve - lop -
of all the heav'n - ly sweet - ness reign - ing In days when you my heart did

ROMANCE

MEDIUM LOW VOICE

Paul Bourget

Claude Debussy
(1862 - 1918)
ed. KEM

L'âme é-va-po-rée et souf-
The soul of fleet-ing and

fran - te, L'â-me dou - ce, l'âme o-do ran - te Des lis di-vins
suff - ering, Soul so gen - tle, O fra-grant scent of li-ly fair,

que j'ai cueil - li Dans le jar-din de ta pen-sée,
that I have gath - ered in the gar-den of your thought,

APRÈS UN RÊVE

After a Dream

MEDIUM HIGH VOICE

Romain Bussine

Gabriel Fauré
(1845 - 1924)
ed. KEM

APRÈS UN RÊVE

After a Dream

MEDIUM LOW VOICE

Romain Bussine

Gabriel Fauré
(1845 - 1924)
ed. KEM

Tu ray - on - nais comme un ciel _____ é - clai - ré par l'au -
All ra - diant thou as the sky _____ at Au - ro - ra's ap -

ro - re; Tu m'ap - pe -
pear - ing I heard you

lais _____ et je quit - tais la ter - re Pour m'en - fuir a - vec
call _____ and to me it was gi - ven to de - part from this

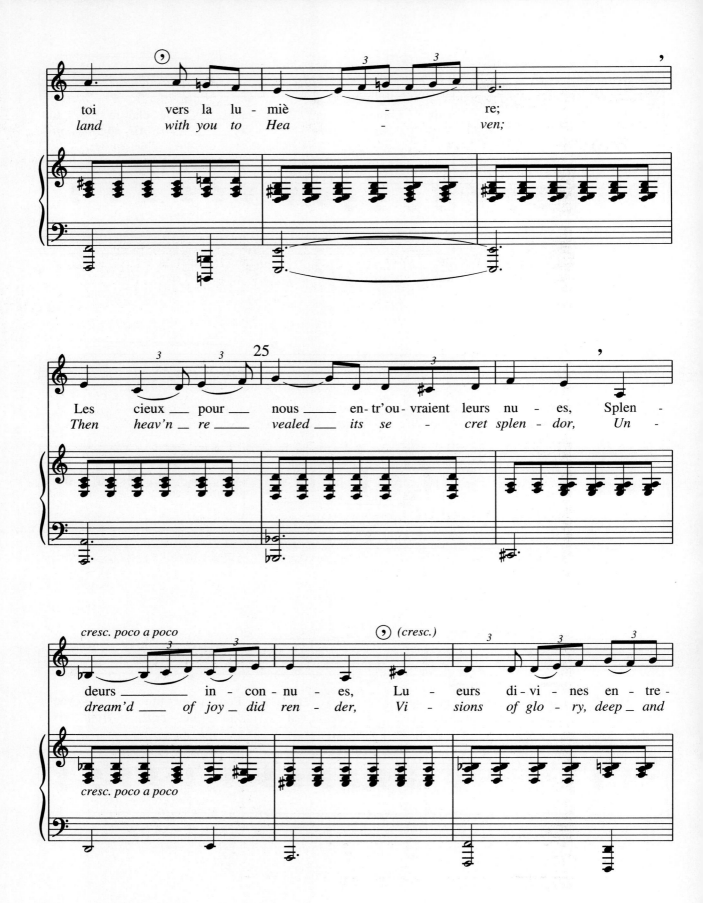

vu - es. Hé - las! Hé - las, tris - te ré - veil _ des
ten - der. A - las, A - las! Sad 'tis to wake _ from

son ges, Je t'ap - pel - le, ô
dream ing! Ah, re - turn, O

nuit, _____ rends - moi tes men - son ges, Re -
night, _____ give me back your il - lu - sions! Re -

viens, re - viens ra - di - eu -
turn, *Re* - *turn* *in* *your* *splen* -

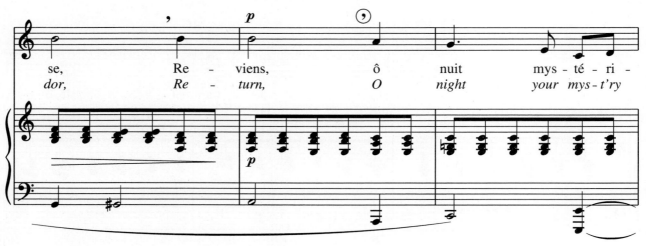

se, Re - viens, ô nuit mys - té - ri -
dor, *Re* - *turn,* *O* *night* *your* *mys - t'ry*

eu - - se!
ten - - *der!*

OBSTINATION

A Resolve

MEDIUM HIGH VOICE

François Coppée
Translation by Constance Bache

H. de Fontenailles
ed. KEM

OBSTINATION

A Resolve

MEDIUM LOW VOICE

François Coppée
Translation by Constance Bache

H. de Fontenailles
ed. KEM

Vous aur-ez beau faire et beau di - re! L'ou-bli me ser-ait o - di-eux,
It is all in vain to im - plore me, Not to let her im - age be-guile,

Et je vois tou-jours son sou-ri - re Des a - dieux, des a-
For her face is ev - er be-fore me, And her smile, and her

L'HEURE EXQUISE

The Exquisite Hour

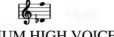

MEDIUM HIGH VOICE

Paul Verlaine

Reynaldo Hahn
(1874 - 1947)
ed. KEM

Ô bien ai - mé - e.
O dear be - lov - ed!

L'é - tang re - flè - te, pro - fond mir - oir, La sil - hou - et -
A faith - ful mir - ror, the pool re - flects, The sil - hou - ette

te du sau - le noir, Où le vent pleu - re. Rê -
of wil - lows black, Where weeps the wind: Oh

C'est   l'heu - re ex -
It   is   the

qui   se.
hour   of   dream - ing!

senza rall.

L'HEURE EXQUISE

The Exquisite Hour

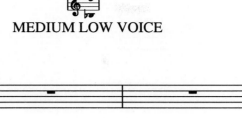

MEDIUM LOW VOICE

Paul Verlaine

Reynaldo Hahn
(1874 - 1947)
ed. KEM

Ô bien ai - mé - e.
O dear be - lov - ed!

L'é-tang re-flè-te, pro-fond mir-oir, La sil-hou-et -
A faith-ful mir-ror, the pool re-flects, The sil-hou-ette

te du sau-le noir, Où le vent pleu - re. Rê -
of wil-lows black, Where weeps the wind: Oh

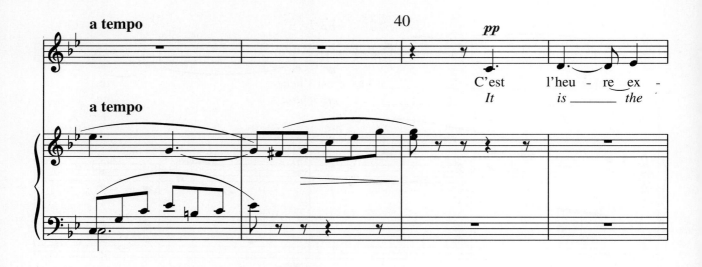

C'est l'heu - re ex -
It is ___ the

qui ___ se.
hour ___ of dream - ing!

BOIS ÉPAIS

Sombre Woods (From *Amadis*)

MEDIUM HIGH VOICE

English text by Thoe. Marzials

Jean Baptiste Lully
(1632 - 1687)
ed. KEM

Bois é - pais re - dou - ble ton om - bre,
Som - bre woods, ye glades dark and lone - ly

Tu ne saur - ais être as - sez som - bre, Tu
Where mid - night gloom en - ters on - ly, Oh!

sens un dés-es-poir Dont l'hor-reur est ex-trê - me,
now this bro-ken heart Nev - er more may en-fold her,

Je ne dois plus voir ce _____ que j'ai - me, Je ne veux
If no more these eyes may _____ be-hold her, Then ev - er

plus souf-frir le jour. _____ Je ne veux
more I hate the light. _____

BOIS ÉPAIS

Sombre Woods (From *Amadis*)

MEDIUM LOW VOICE

English text by Thoe. Marzials

Jean Baptiste Lully
(1632 - 1687)
ed. KEM

Bois é - pais re - dou - ble ton om - bre,
Som - bre woods, ye glades dark and lone - ly

Tu ne saur - ais être as - sez som - bre, Tu
Where mid - night gloom en - ters on - ly, Oh!

mal-heur-eux___ a-mour, Je sens un dés-es-poir Dont l'hor-

your un-bound___ed night, If now this bro-ken heart Nev-er

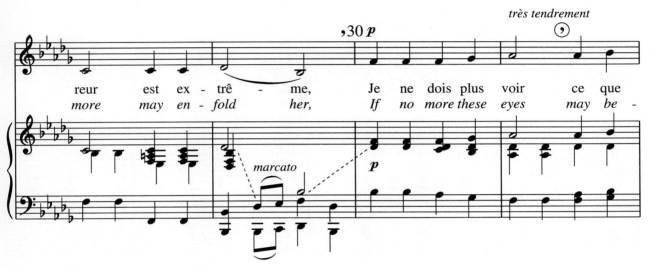

reur est ex-trê-me, Je ne dois plus voir ce que

more may en-fold her, If no more these eyes may be-

j'ai-me, Je ne veux plus souf-frir le jour, Je

hold her, Then ev-er more I hate the light, If

sens un dés-es-poir   Dont l'hor-reur   est ex-trê – me,
now this bro-ken heart   Nev – er   more   may en-fold   her,

Je ne dois plus voir   ce___ que___ j'ai – me,   Je ne veux
If   no more these eyes   may___ be – hold   her,   Then ev – er

plus souf-frir   le   jour.___
more I   hate   the   light.___

LIBERA ME

Deliver Me, O Lord (From *Requiem*)

MEDIUM HIGH VOICE

Gabriel Fauré
(1845 - 1924)

LATIN SONGS

la: Quan - do coe - li mo - ven - di sunt: Quan - do coe - li
tri - al;   then shall heav - en and earth be moved, then shall heav'n and

mo - ven - di sunt et ter - ra;   Dum ve - ne - ris ju - di -
earth be con - sumed to - geth - er,   for thou ___ shalt come, thou shalt

ca - re sae - cu - lum per ig - nem. ___
come ___ up - on the earth in judg - ment. ___

LIBERA ME

Deliver Me, O Lord (From *Requiem*)

MEDIUM LOW VOICE

Gabriel Fauré
(1845 - 1924)

PIE JESU

Blessed Jesus (From *Requiem*)

MEDIUM HIGH VOICE

Gabriel Fauré
(1845 - 1924)
ed. KEM

PIE JESU

Blessed Jesus (From *Requiem*)

MEDIUM LOW VOICE

Gabriel Fauré
(1845 - 1924)
ed. KEM

BENEDICTUS

(Excerpt From *Mass in G*)

MEDIUM HIGH VOICE

Blessed is He Who comes in the name of the Lord.

Franz Schubert
(1797 - 1828)
edited by Alice Parker
and Robert Shaw

Be - ne - dic - tus qui ve - nit in no - mi-ne Do - mi - ni, be - ne -

BENEDICTUS

(Excerpt From *Mass in G*)

MEDIUM LOW VOICE
Blessed is He Who comes in the name of the Lord.

Franz Schubert
(1797 - 1828)
edited by Alice Parker
and Robert Shaw

QUI SEDES AD DEXTERAM

From *Gloria*

MEDIUM HIGH VOICE

You, Who sit at the right hand of the Father, have mercy on us.

Antonio Vivaldi
(c. 1675 - 1741)

mi - se - re - re, mi - se - re - re _____ no - bis.

Qui se - des ad dex - te - ram Pa -

tris, mi - se - re -

re no bis,

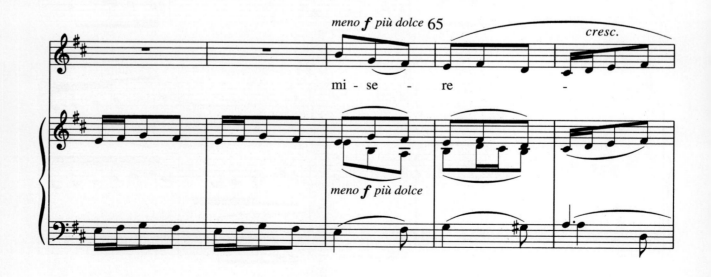

mi - se - re -

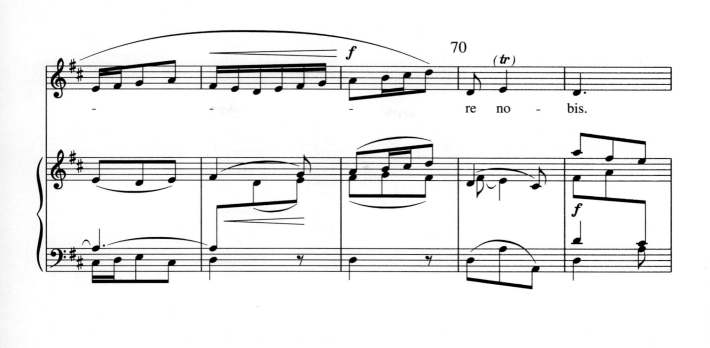

re no - bis.

Qui se -

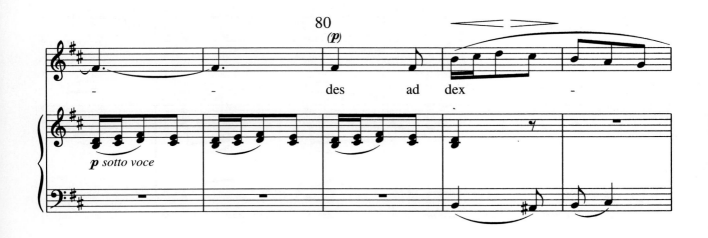

des ad dex -

re - re _____ no - bis,

mi - se - re - re, mi - se - re - re, mi - se -

re - re _____ no - bis.

QUI SEDES AD DEXTERAM

From *Gloria*

MEDIUM LOW VOICE

You, Who sit at the right hand of the Father, have mercy on us.

Antonio Vivaldi
(c. 1675 - 1741)

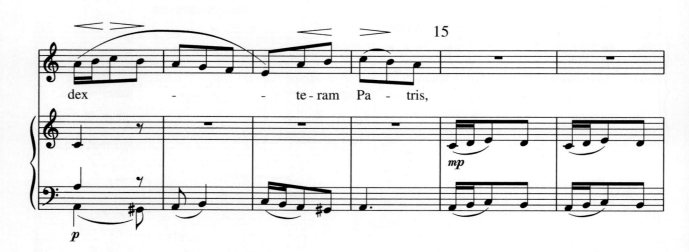

mi – se – re – – – – – – – re, – – – – – re,

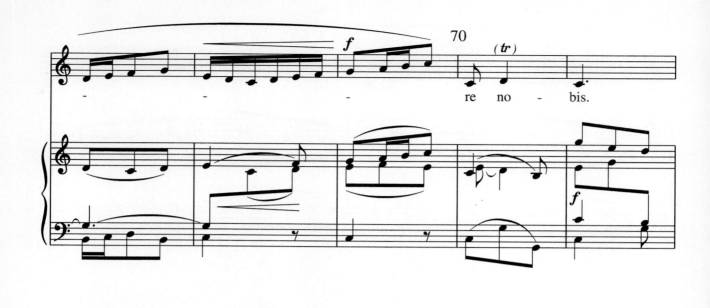

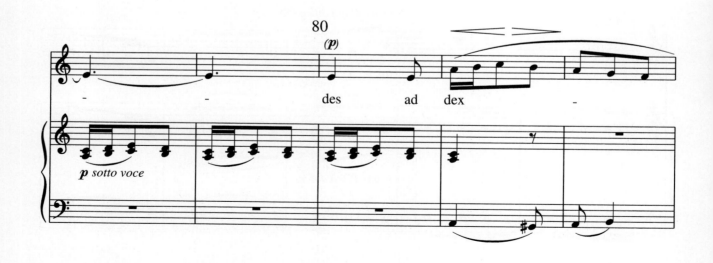

Interpretive Comments
About the Music

ENGLISH SONGS

Have You Seen But a White Lillie Grow? – **Anonymous**

This song by an unknown composer is set to a poem by Ben Jonson (1573–1637) about a beloved one's beauty. The poem has two different versions, one using the word "white," as in this edition, and the other using "bright." Although "white" is the more frequent version, the choice is up to the singer. The original poem is included in *Ben Jonson*, vol. 8, eds. C.H.H. Percy and E. Simpson (Oxford University Press, 1954), and that source has been consulted during the preparation of this edition.

This is an interesting Old English text, and should be sung with a certain simplicity. Particular attention should be given to clarity of diction, for the singer must sing with some agility. An excellent study song, it is also well suited to studio or recital performance.

Blow, Blow, Thou Winter Wind – **Arne**

Thomas Arne (1710–1778) considered entering the practice of law, but he studied music privately and made it his profession. He wrote a large number of operas and other works for the stage as well as oratorios and instrumental compositions. "Blow, Blow, Thou Winter Wind" was written for a revival of Shakespeare's *As You Like It* in 1740. The original key was probably B flat. The text expresses the feelings of a group of exiled men who are homeless at winter time. The music should move at about 116 quarter notes. The phrases in this song are not long, and most singers will enjoy the simple, straightforward character of the music.

Shenandoah – **arranged by C. Dougherty**

This American folk song, also known as "Across the Wide Missouri," has long been a favorite with singers. It has been sung on recital programs, in choral arrangements, and by folk singers. Described as a sea chanty or work song, "Shenandoah" may be sung in various ways, and this arrangement is often performed. The melody and shifting rhythms make it very appealing music for study and performance. The music should generally begin rather quietly and build toward the end of the verse. The text expresses a deep yearning for home. Although the interpretation of folk music should remain an individual decision, the tempo of this arrangement should be kept steady except for a slight *ritard* at the end of each verse. This *ritard* is to be broadened at the very end of the composition.

The song contains mixed meters (C, 3/4 , etc.), and the singer will be well advised to keep the quarter notes even.

Oh Sleep, Why Dost Thou Leave Me? (from *Semele*) – Handel

George F. Handel composed many Italian operas and oratorios while in England, and his compositions in both forms were quite successful. This edition is from the Handel Society Edition as edited by Friedrich Chrysander, with the piano part realized by E. F. Richter. The singer's and bass parts are as originally composed by Handel, and the remaining notes in the piano accompaniment have been included essentially as realized by Richter. Composed in 1743 and first performed the next year, it was called "Story of Semele" because the music was not considered to be truly an oratorio or opera. However, it is now more generally considered to be closer to the style of an oratorio.

In "Oh Sleep, Why Dost Thou Leave Me?" Semele, a princess of Thebes, cannot sleep and wishes for a dream in which her beloved will return. Some of the phrases may be long for undergraduate singers, but Baroque practice allows some use of alternate phrasing. This music should be sung with a full, mature sound, and there should be no thought of hurrying. The final phrase of the vocal line ("restore" m.24) provides an excellent opportunity to build to a full, dramatic climax. The original key was given by Chrysander as E major.

The tempo should be moderately slow and steady. The necessary breath control and sustained, legato singing may be a challenge for beginners. More performers will welcome the challenge of performing this music in a mature, natural style. The opening phrase (measures 5–7) may be performed ad lib.

Down Among the Dead Men – Old English Air

This anonymous drinking song is generally sung by men. The music has a strong pulse, and the vocal range is not wide. It can be assigned to a student during the early months of vocal study. The hearty character of the music and text makes it an attractive study song. The final measures of the last verse should be sung more broadly to give a greater sense of the song's conclusion.

Dido's Lament (from *Dido and Aeneas*) – Purcell

Henry Purcell (1659–1695) was appointed composer-in-residence for the king's violins in 1677, and in 1679 he succeeded his teacher, John Blow, as organist of Westminster Abbey. He was appointed organist of the Royal Chapel in 1682, and this appointment was renewed by James II (1685) and William II (1689). The final royal occasion for which he provided music was the funeral of Queen Mary in 1695. He was buried in Westminster Abbey during the same year.

The recitative and aria, "Dido's Lament," is a foremost example of seventeenth century English opera, and this music continues to be frequently performed. The text is about love and death, and the singer must give importance to every note and word. Dido, Queen of Carthage, takes her own life and asks at the close that she be remembered. The opera was first performed at a girls' boarding school in Chelsea, and its story is based on the *Aeneid*.

This recitative can serve as excellent study material for a student to learn to interpret such music. It is recommended that the singer adhere strictly to the written notation at first and allow more freedom to emerge naturally as a more mature interpretation develops.

The aria, too, serves as excellent music for study and performance. Of course, the recitative and aria are to be performed together. If the singer understands the text fully, it will follow that a full tone will be used. Every note is important, the music moves slowly and majestically, and clear enunciation is essential. Only those female singers who can sing with this kind of tone and clarity of enunciation should include this music in their repertory for public performance.

I Attempt From Love's Sickness to Fly (from *The Indian Queen*) – Purcell

Henry Purcell (1659–1695) was perhaps the most gifted English composer of his time. He wrote in nearly every medium, and his operas include the well known *Dido and Aeneas* (1689). His songs are particularly effective because of his ability to adapt the melody to the text. The florid passages, in particular, are not simply for vocal display; they are to heighten the drama of a particular word or phrase, as is seen in this song. Purcell uses melismatic passages, for example, when the text contains the word "fly" (measures 11–12, 34–35, and 59–60), and this florid setting virtually requires the singer to make the text sound authentic.

The song is to be performed with lightness of vocal tone and clarity of diction. Careful attention to phrasing and the Old English style will also add character. The text simply deals with an inability to escape the grasp of Cupid, and both singer and pianist are to keep the music moving. Each succeeding section is to be sung with more fullness of tone and somewhat slower tempo, but nowhere should there be any hint of heaviness. It is a light-hearted song which performers and audiences often enjoy, and it serves as an excellent study song for students who are working to improve their diction and execution of the florid style.

The introduction and interlude have been added to the original music.

O Mistress Mine – Quilter

Roger Quilter (1877–1953) is best known for his songs, most of which were written between 1900 and 1930. His style was seemingly effortless and quite sensitive, and his excellence consisted of doing what several other English composers did but with better taste.

He composed several settings of Shakespeare's works starting in 1905; three of these were settings of "O Mistress Mine." His style was conservative, and his songs have exhibited a natural melodic line supported by a colorful accompaniment. This setting may appear to be more sentimental than necessary as the final line is repeated, but Quilter was quite effective in employing a strophic form which was able to serve well the different poetic meanings found in the poem.

Simple Gifts ('Tis the Gift to Be Simple) – Shaker Tune

This well-known Shaker song is often performed. The tune has been quoted by composers, most notably by Aaron Copland in "Appalachian Spring."

"Simple Gifts" is a song about simpler times and a "plainer" style of living. The music is not complex, and the vocal range is just an octave. Although the song may be performed by a singer of considerable experience, it also serves as a fine study song for the beginning student.

The Shakers were a religious group which migrated from England in about 1774.

They advocated equality of the sexes, celibacy, and communal ownership of property. They were noted for their neat, peaceful villages, pure architecture, fine craftsmanship, and their distinctive songs, dances, and rituals. By the 1970's, the sect was virtually extinct.

Pretty Ring Time – Warlock

Peter Warlock (1894–1930) was a self-taught English composer. Under his original name of Philip Heseltine, he wrote about music and edited English works of the Elizabethan era. Using the name Peter Warlock, he produced many songs and choral compositions; he also composed some instrumental music.

This text was taken from the writings of Shakespeare and has been given a colorful setting. The text concerns the feelings of young lovers in springtime. There are several meter changes in the music, but they fall quite naturally. The notes move quickly and there are no long sustained notes.

Understanding the text is quite important if one is to fully enjoy this song, and the singer needs to take care to project its meaning clearly. Although this song should be performed by a singer of some musical background, it is interesting music which performers and audiences alike will enjoy when it is performed with the desired motion and lightheartedness.

ITALIAN SONGS

Sebben, crudele (Savage and Heartless) – Caldara

Antonio Caldara (1670–1736) was a pupil of Legrenzi and was an Italian composer. He became Vice-Kapellmeister at the Imperial Court, Vienna, in 1716. Caldara wrote more than 100 operas and oratorios; he also wrote many songs and other works.

This music moves gracefully. The text is primarily concerned with expressing steadfast love even though there is scorn placed on the one who continues to love. The vocal line is to be sung legato, and the music moves deliberately. Each note is important and embellishments are included in the vocal line to add to important moments. The vocal line often moves by step, and each section has a clearly defined focal point. The music has much variety when compared to other Italian art songs of the same time period.

Sebben, crudele, mi fai languir,	seb-bɛn krudɛle mi fai laŋgwir
sempre fedele ti voglio amar.	sɛmpre fedele ti vɔʎo amar
Con la lunghezza del mio servir	kon la lunget-sa dɛl mio sɛrvir
la tua fierezza saprò stancar.	la tua fjeret-sa saprɔ staŋkar

Vittoria, mio core! (Victorious, my heart is!) – Carissimi

Giacomo Carissimi (1605–1674) was an Italian composer, singer, and organist. His chief position was as *maestro di capella* at the Jesuit Collegio Germanico, Rome, where he remained until his death. He became a priest in 1637.

Carissimi is best known as a composer of vocal music, and his oratorio *Jepthe* is recognized as a foremost example of Italian oratorio of this time. He taught many young musicians who later became well known; they included such composers as A. Scarlatti, Cesti, and the Frenchman, Charpentier.

"Vittoria, mio core!" is often studied and performed, especially by male singers. It is to be sung at a bright tempo in order to achieve the proper mood, and its musical and vocal requirements place it among the moderately difficult art songs. It should be sung by a singer who has a full, resonant voice and one who has control over the full dynamic range. Also the singer should be able to perform the melismas easily and fluently.

Vittoria, mio core! non lagrimar più,	vit-tɔrja mio kɔre non lagrimar pju
è sciolta d'Amore la vil servitù.	ɛ ʃɔlta damore la vil sɛrvitu
Già l'empia a' tuoi danni	dʒa lempja twɔi danni
fra stuolo di sguardi,	fra stwɔlo di zgwardi
con vezzi bugiardi dispose gl'inganni;	kon vet-si budʒardi dispoʒe ʎiŋgan ni
le frode, gli affanni non hanno più loco,	le frɔde ʎaf-fan-ni non an-no pju lɔko
del crudo suo foco è spento l'ardore!	dɛl krudo suo fɔko ɛ spento lardore
Da luci ridenti non esce più strale,	da lutʃi ridɛnti non ɛʃe pju strale
che piaga mortale nel petto m'avventi:	ke pjaga mortale nɛl pɛt-to mav-vɛnti
nel duol, ne' tormenti io più non mi sfaccio	nɛl dwɔl ne tɔrmenti io pju non mi sfat-ʃo
è rotto ogni laccio, sparito il timore!	ɛ rottoɲi lat-ʃo sparito il timore

Vergin, tutto amor (Virgin, full of love) – Durante

Francesco Durante (1684–1755) was an Italian composer active in Naples and Rome; he probably also went abroad. He was known as the best teacher of composition in Naples, and Pergolesi was among his students. Durante wrote no operas, but he became known for his sacred dramas and secular and sacred cantatas. He found fame more through his sacred compositions, which also included masses, motets, and psalms.

"Vergin, tutto amor" first appeared without words as an exercise piece for students. The text, a eulogy to the Virgin Mary, was added years later. The song should be interpreted as a sinner's prayer for mercy, to be sung with reverance and understanding. There should be considerable emphasis on legato singing as well as on a certain recognizable restraint. While this music is to be studied by a singer who has already sung other songs in Italian, it is often included as repertory for study and recital performance.

Vergin, tutto amor, O Madre di bontade,	verdʒin tutto amor o madre di bontade
o Madre pia, ascolta, dolce Maria,	o madre pia askolta doltʃe maria
la voce del peccator.	la votʃe dɛl pek kator
Il pianto suo ti muova,	il pjanto suo ti mwɔva
giungano a te i suoi lamenti,	dʒuŋgano a te i swɔi lamenti
suo duol, suoi tristi accenti	suo dwɔl swɔi tristi atʃenti
oda pietoso quel tuo cor.	oda pjetozo kwɛl tuo kɔr

O del mio dolce ardor (O Thou Belov'd) – Gluck

This composition is more difficult than most of the Italian songs in this section. The tempo is moderate, the vocal line is to be performed legato, and careful control of the breath is required. The vocal range is an octave and a fifth, and the intervals in the vocal line occur up to an octave. The music is in three-part form, and every note is important. This aria is recommended for performance by a singer who possesses the technical ability and artistic sensitivity to communicate at this level.

This music was originally sung by Paride in Gluck's third opera, *Paride ed Elena* (1770); of Gluck's first three operas, this one was received least well. The complete opera is generally no longer performed, but this aria remains a valued composition in the singer's repertoire.

O del mio dolce ardor bramato oggetto,	o dɛl mio doltʃe ardor bramato odʒetto
L'aura che tu respiri, alfin respiro,	laura ke tu respiri alfin respiro
Ovunque il guardo io giro,	ovuŋkwe il gwardo io dʒiro

Le tue vaghe sembianze	le tue vage sɛmbjɑntse
Amore in me dipinge:	amore in me dipindʒe
Il mio pensier si finge	il mio pɛnsjɛr si findʒe
Le più liete speranze;	le pju ljete sperɑntse
E nel desio che così m'empie il petto	e nel dezio ke kozi mempje il pɛtto
Cerco te, chiamo te, spero e sospiro. Ah!	tʃɛrko te kjamo te spero e sospiro ɑ

Ah, mio cor (Ah! My Heart) – Handel

George F. Handel (1685–1759) was an English composer of German birth, and he composed many operas in Italian style. Handel played violin and harpsichord at the Hamburg opera when he was eighteen years old, and his operas *Almira* and *Nero* were performed there by 1705. The next year he accepted an invitation to go to Italy for three years. During that time, he had his operas and dramatic works performed in Florence, Rome, Naples, and Venice.

In 1718–19 a group of English noblemen, who had received royal support, launched the Royal Academy of Music with Handel as music director. The Academy opened in 1720 and many of Handel's operas were performed there. (He turned to composing oratorios when his operas were no longer well received.) *Alcina*, in which this aria appears, dates from 1735, and this music is sung by the mighty "Alcina" herself.

"Ah, mio cor" is one of Handel's more often performed arias. It is valuable music for study or performance, and this edition was prepared after examining the score in the *Handel Collected Edition*. The motion of this music is conducive to improving the singer's ability to sing a legato line, and the singer must also be able to successfully negotiate intervals up to an octave. The dramatic content of the text can best be communicated by singing with clear diction and careful attention to dynamics. The original accompaniment was for keyboard and strings.

Ah! mio cor, schernito sei.	ɑ mio kɔr skɛrnito sɛi
Stelle, Dei, Nume d'amore! traditore,	stel le dɛi nume damore traditore
T'amo tanto, puoi lasciarmi sola in pianto?	tamo tanto pwɔi laʃarmi sola in pjanto
Oh! Dei! puoi lasciarmi, perchè?	o dɛi pwɔi laʃarmi pɛrke

Ombra mai fù (from Serse) – Handel

This is one of the best known Handel arias, and was originally included in the opera *Serse*. The music moves deliberately and majestically; it gives the singer authentic opportunities to approach initial attacks in various ways and provides many opportunities for young singers to increase vocal control. Some phrases begin softly and build while others are to be started with a full tone. The entire aria is to be sung quite legato, and it serves as very good music to help a beginning student work on refining breath control. The vocal range is an octave and a fourth, and the music provides the student with numerous opportunities to work to develop both technically and artistically.

Ombra mai fù di vegetabile,	ombra mai fu di vedʒetabile
Cara ed amabile, soave più.	kara ed amabile soave pju

Lasciatemi morire! (Let Me Die!) – Monteverdi

Claudio Monteverdi (1567–1643) published several books of Italian madrigals and motets, and he came to be recognized as an important advocate of a more modern approach to harmony and textual expression. The opera *Arianna*, from which this music has been taken, was first produced in 1608. This lament is the only music from *Arianna* to be often performed today, and it can help a student learn basic requirements of performing dramatic Baroque vocal music.

"Lasciatemi morire!" moves slowly and majestically. An increasing fullness of tone and a sense of anguish are to increasingly lead toward the phrase "in cosi gran martire." The pause which follows should not be minimized. The vocal range is an octave, and, while the singer should be capable of performing with a full, dark tone quality, this music is within the grasp of most student singers. It is recommended that public performance be undertaken only by singers who are capable of communicating the emotions of anguish and torment.

Lasciatemi morire!	laʃatemi morire
e che volete che mi conforte	e ke volete ke mi konfɔrte
in così dura sorte,	in kozi dura sɔrte
in così gran martire?	in kozi gran martire

Se tu m'ami (If Thou Lov'st Me) – Pergolesi

Although Giovanni Pergolesi (1710–1736) was only moderately well known during his lifetime, history has shown him to have been a leading composer in the rise of Italian comic opera. His works include opera, sacred music, chamber cantatas, duets, songs, and some instrumental music. Because some compositions have been attributed to him incorrectly, there may be some question as to whether he actually composed this song.

The tempo should not be fast, but this attractive and unusual song must have good motion. Some freedom of tempo is appropriate, and the slowing of tempo, where marked, may be a little broader than in some other compositions of this time. The text expresses a sense of pity and pain, but such thoughts are not to be taken too seriously. The performers should take particular care to communicate the delightful sense of humor expressed in this music.

Se tu m'ami, se tu sospiri	se tu mami se tu sospiri
Sol per me, gentil pastor,	sol per me dʒentil pastor
Ho dolor de' tuoi martiri,	o dolor de twɔi martiri
Ho diletto del tuo amor,	o dilɛtto dɛl tuo amor
Ma se pensi che soletto	ma se pɛnsi ke solet to
Io ti debba riamar,	io ti deb ba riamar
Pastorello, sei soggetto	pastorɛllo sɛi sodʒet to
Facilmente a t'ingannar.	fatʃilmente a tiŋgan nar
Bella rosa porporina	bɛl la rɔza pɔrporina
Oggi Silvia sceglierà,	ɔdʒi silvja ʃeʎera
Con la scusa della spina	kon la skuza del la spina
Doman poi la sprezzerà.	doman pɔi la spretsera
Ma degli uomini il consiglio	ma deʎi wɔmini il konsiʎo
Io per me non seguirò.	io per me non segwirɔ
Non perchè mi piace il giglio	non pɛrke mi pjatʃe il dʒiʎo
Gli altri fiori sprezzerò.	ʎaltri fjori spretserɔ

Se Florindo è fedele (If Florindo Be Constant) – Scarlatti

Alessandro Scarlatti (1660–1725) was a Baroque composer who studied in Rome, became court conductor at Naples (1684–1702), and composed operas for Ferdinando (III) de Medici. He was also appointed choirmaster of S. Maria Maggiore in Rome and music director to Cardinal Pietro Ottoboni. He held posts in Naples and was considered to have been the most prolific composer of Italian operas during his time. In addition to some 115 operas, he composed many oratorios, cantatas, masses, passions, motets, concertos, chamber music, and compositions for the harpsichord.

"Se Florindo è fedele" can best be performed by musicians who have had some previous experience. This is a love song that moves rather quickly, and the singer is advised to exercise restraint before utilizing a full sound at the climactic point just before the end. The singer and accompanist should keep the music moving with a certain lightness and agility.

Se Florindo è fedele io m'innamorerò,	se florindo ε fedele io min-namorerɔ
s'è fedele Florindo m'innamorerò.	sε fedele florindo min namorero
Potrà ben l'arco tendere il faretrato arcier,	potra bεn larko tεndere il farεtrato artʃεr
ch'io mi saprò difendere d'un guardo lusinghier.	kio mi saprɔ difεndere dun gwardo luziŋgjεr
Preghi, pianti e querele, io non ascolterò,	prεgi pjanti e kwεrεle io non askolterɔ
ma se sarà fedele io m'innamorerò.	ma se sara fedele io min-namorerɔ

Tu lo sai (You Know Quite Well) – Torelli

Giuseppe Torelli (1658–1709) studied in Bologna and in 1686 joined the S. Petronio orchestra as a violinist. His reputation was as a violin virtuoso. In 1696–99 he was at the Ansbach court and then went to Vienna before returning to Bologna, where he was violinist at S. Petronio again.

He composed about 150 instrumental works and contributed significantly to the development of the concerto grosso and solo concerto. He also wrote oratorio, art songs, and some other vocal works. The text of this song was also set by Pietro P. Bencini (c. 1670–1755).

"Tu lo sai" is a love song which contains an element of hurt brought on by an unfaithful lover. It is a song which has long been studied and sung on studio and public recital programs.

Tu lo sai quanto t'amai	tu lo sai kwanto tamai
tu lo sai, lo sai, crudel!	tu lo sai lo sai krudεl
Io non bramo altra mercé,	io non bramo altra mεrtʃe
Ma ricordati di me,	ma rikordati di me
E poi sprezza un infedel!	e pɔi sprεtsa un infedεl

GERMAN SONGS

Ich liebe dich so wie du mich (I Love Thee) – Beethoven

Ludwig van Beethoven (1770–1827) is well known as one of the most performed and original composers. His nine symphonies and other instrumental compositions are among the most important orchestral compositions. His vocal music performances are most often of his opera, *Fidelio*, and large choral compositions, but Beethoven also composed significant music for the solo singer.

Beethoven's first public appearance in Vienna was in 1795 as a pianist and composer. As a composer, he worked tirelessly until the last revision of the music satisfied him. He had an enormous influence on the course of 19th century art music.

"Ich liebe dich so wie du mich" has also been published under the titles "Zärtliche Liebe" (Tender Love) and "Ich liebe dich" (I Love Thee). The *Beethoven Werke*, Abteilung XII, Band I (1990) was consulted during the preparation of this edition, and such differences as may appear in the text or vocal line are because other editions may differ from that source.

This song has a certain sincerity and depth of feeling along with purity and simplicity. A legato vocal line and clarity of diction are important to unlocking the proper nobility and beauty found in this music. Beethoven's ideals are shown in the text he chose, and yet the music is rather simple, almost folk-like. The text begins with stanza two of a poem by Carl Herrosee. The song was first published in 1800.

Ich liebe dich, so wie du mich,	ɪç libə dɪç zo vi du mɪç
am Abend und am Morgen,	am abənt ʊnt am mɔrgən
noch war kein Tag, wo du und ich	nɔx var kæn tak vo du ʊnt mɪç
nicht teilten uns're Sorgen.	nɪçt tælten ʊnzrə zɔrgən
Auch waren sie für dich und mich	aox varən zi fyr dɪç ʊnt mɪç
geteilt leicht zu ertragen;	gətælt læçt tsu ɛrtragən
du tröstetest im Kummer mich,	du trøstətəst ɪm kʊmmər mɪç
ich weint' in deine Klagen.	ɪç vænt ɪn dænə klagən
Drum Gottes Segen über dir,	drʊm gɔtəs zegən ybər dir
du meines Lebens Freude,	du mænəs lebəns frɔødə
Gott schütze dich, erhalt' dich mir,	gɔt ʃytsə dɪç ɛrhalt dɪç mir
schütz' und erhalt' uns beide!	ʃyts ʊnt ɛrhalt ʊns bædə

Still wie die Nacht (Still as the Night) – Bohm

This song is often used as a study song and is to be performed in a sustained, legato manner. It serves as excellent study material for beginning students who are working to control their breath and to develop a full, controlled tone at the different dynamic levels. While optional breath marks are included, students are encouraged to take the longer phrase as often as possible. Also, care is to be taken not to detract from the *con moto* portion (m. 36) by starting the *ritard* too soon. The accompaniment is to be kept smooth and always moving forward, and the tempo *must* not drag.

Still wie die Nacht, tief wie das Meer,	ʃtɪl vi di naxt tif vi das mer
soll deine Liebe sein!	zɔl dænə li bə zæn
Wenn du mich liebst so wie ich dich,	vɛn du mɪç lipst zo vi ɪç dɪç
will ich dein eigen sein.	vɪl ɪç dæn ægən zæn
Heiss wie der Stahl und fest wie der Stein	hæs vi der ʃtal ʊnt fɛst vi der ʃtæn
soll deine Liebe sein!	zɔl dænə libə zæn

Sapphische Ode (Sapphic Ode) – Brahms

Johannes Brahms (1833–1897) was the son of a doublebass player at the Hamburg Stadttheater. His earliest compositions were songs and piano compositions. It is often said that his music reflects both the austerity of his north German home and the charm of Vienna. He was also influenced by gypsy music and German folksong. This is one of his best known art songs, and *Ein deutsches Requiem* is his most cited choral composition.

"Sapphische Ode" may be more difficult to perform than it first appears. Although short, the syncopation in the accompaniment and some intervals in the vocal line can present difficulties for beginning students. Many performers find that the phrasing falls more naturally if the tempo is taken slightly brighter than as marked in the music, and the song should be sung with a strong sense of legato. A few phrases are long, and singers may need to give more than the usual amount of attention to perfecting the rhythm and intervals. Also, the chromatic movement may cause some problems. The text deals initially with the beauty of roses at night, and the second verse compares roses with kisses shared with a sweetheart. This song should be sung with tenderness so as to reflect the warmth found in the text.

Rosen brach ich Nachts mir am dunklen Hage;
süsser hauchten Duft sie, als je am Tage;
doch verstreuten reich die bewegten Äste
Tau, der mich nässte.
Auch der Küsse Duft mich wie nie berückte,
die ich nachts vom Strauch deiner Lippen pflückte:
doch auch dir, bewegt im Gemüt gleich jenen,
tauten die Tränen.

rozən brax ıç naxts mir am dʊŋklən hagə
zysər haoxtən dʊft zi als je am tagə
dɔx fɛrʃtrɔøtən ræç di bəvektən ɛstə
tao der mıç nɛstə
aox der kysə dʊft mıç vi ni bəryktə
di ıç naxts fɔm ʃtraox dænər lıpən pflyktə
dɔx aox dir bəvekt ım gəmyt glæə jenən
taotən di trenən

Gute Nacht (Good Night) – Franz

Robert Franz (1815–1892) composed more than 250 songs and much other music. His interest in the vocal music of Bach and Handel caused him to write additional accompaniments to several of their passions, oratorios, and other works. Deafness and nervousness have been given as the reason for him retiring in 1868.

"Gute Nacht" is a lyric song which is also quite sustained. The accompaniment is primarily a reiterated rhythmic pattern and is not technically difficult. The vocal range is an octave, and this song can be given to a singer who has had little training. However, this song is sophisticated enough to be included on recital programs. When performers build the phrases with consistent motion, the music has an attractive quality that appeals to performers and audiences.

Die Höh'n und Wälder schon steigen
immer tiefer ins Abendgold,
ein Vöglein fragt in den Zweigen:
ob es Liebchen grüssen sollt'?
O Voglein, du hast dich betrogen,
sie wohnet nicht mehr im Tal,
schwing' auf dich zum Himmel's bogen,
gruss' sie droben zum letzten mal.

di høn unt vɛldər ʃon ʃtægən
ımər tifər ıns abɛntgɔlt
æn føglæn frakt ın den tswægən
ɔp ɛs libçən grysən zɔlt
o foglæn du hast dıç bətrogən
zi vonət nıçt mɛr ım tal
ʃving aof dıç tsum hımməls bogən
grus zi drobən tsum lɛtstən mal

Ungeduld (Impatience) – Schubert

Franz Schubert (1797–1828) composed more than 600 art songs, and his music is always included in the German repertory. This song, which is number seven in the song cycle, *Die schöne Müllerin*, is frequently performed by itself. The complete cycle contains twenty songs and was composed in 1823.

This love song is more suited for singers who have had some performing experience. The song builds to the third measure before the first ending, and a singer of some maturity is required to communicate the full meaning. Since "Ungeduld" is strophic, the final climactic point should be left to the last verse. Verse three of the original four has not been included here.

1. Ich schnitt' es gern in alle Rinden ein,
   ich grüb es gern in jeden Kieselstein,
   ich möcht es sä'n auf jedes frische Beet
   mit Kressensamen, der es schnell verrät,
   auf jeden weissen Zettel möcht ich's schreiben:

   ıç ʃnit ɛs gɛrn ın allə rındən æn
   ıç gryp ɛs gɛrn ın jedən ki zəlʃtæn
   ıç møçt ɛs zen aof je dəs frıʃə bet
   mıt kresənzamən der ɛs ʃnel fɛrret
   aof jedən væsən tsetəl møçt ıçs ʃræbən

(Refrain)

Dein ist mein Herz, dein ist mein Herz
und soll es ewig, ewig bleiben!

dæn ıst mæn hɛrts dæn ıst mæn hɛrts
ʊnt zɔl ɛs e vıç e vıç blæbən

2. Ich möcht mir ziehen einen jungen Staar,
bis dass er spräch die Worte rein und klar,
bis er sie spräch mit meines Mundes Klang,
mit meines Herzens vollem, heissen Drang;
dann säng er hell durch ihre Fensterscheiben:

ıç møçt mir tsiən ænən juŋən ʃtar
bıs das er ʃprɛç di vɔrtə ræn ʊnt klar
bıs er zi ʃprɛç mıt mænəs mʊndəs klaŋ
mıt mænəs hɛrtsəns fɔlləm hæsən draŋ
dan zɛŋ er hɛl dʊrç irə fɛnstərʃæbən

3. Ich meint, es müsst in meinen Augen stehn,
auf meinen Wangen müsst man's brennen sehn,
zu lessen wär's auf meinen stummen Mund,
ein jeder Atemzug gäb's laut ihr kund;
und sie merkt nichts von all dem bangen Treiben.

ıç mænt ɛs myst ın mænən ɑogən ʃten
ɑof mænən vaŋən myst mans brennən zen
tsu le zən vɛrs ɑof mænən ʃtʊmmən mʊnt
æn jeder atəmtsuk gɛps lɑot ir kʊnt
ʊnt zi mɛrkt nıçts fɔn al dem baŋən træbən

Du bist wie eine Blume (Thou Art Just Like a Flower) – Schumann

Robert Schumann (1810–1856) developed both musical and literary interests as a young person. He studied law at the university, and also studied piano and harmony with Friedrich Wieck. He later gave up his law studies for music. In 1832 an injury to his right hand caused him to rule out the possibility of pursuing a career as a pianist. In 1833 he founded the *Neue Zeitschrift für Musik* (New Music Journal), and in 1840 he married Clara Wieck, who became a renowned interpreter of his music. He wrote much instrumental and vocal music, and this song is often sung.

Several composers have set the text of "Du bist wie eine Blume" and Schumann's setting is among the most beautiful. The vocal line should be sung quite legato to express a quiet, reflective mood. The vocal range is less than an octave, and the phrase lengths are within the capability of most singers. The song is not technically difficult, but achieving a mature interpretation of the music and text may take some time.

Du bist wie eine blume,
so hold und schön und rein;
ich schau' dich an und Wehmuth
schleicht mir in's Herz hinein.
Mir ist, als ob ich die Hände
auf's Haupt dir legen sollt',
betend, dass Gott dich erhalte
so rein und schön und hold.

du bıst vi ænə blumə
zo hɔlt ʊnt ʃøn ʊnt ræn
ıç ʃɑo dıç an ʊnt ve mʊt
ʃlæçt mir ıns hɛrts hınæn
mir ıst als ɔp ıç di hɛndə
ɑofs hɑopt dir legən zɔlt
betənt das gɔt dıç ɛrhaltə
zo ræn ʊnt ʃøn ʊnt hɔlt

Ich grolle nicht (I'll Not Complain) – Schumann

"Ich grolle nicht" is the seventh song in the cycle, *Dichterliebe*. The music becomes more dramatic as the song progresses, and the climactic point in the text is reached with "ich sah, mein Lieb, wie sehr du elend bist" (I saw how all forlorn thou art, my love). While the dynamic level then becomes softer, the intensity should be maintained to the very end. Also, it should be noted that the optional high notes in measures 27 to 29 were added by the composer. This music is studied often and will undoubtedly continue to be sung at recitals for many years to come.

Ich grolle nicht, und wenn das Herz auch bricht,
ewig verlor'nes Lieb, ich grolle nicht.
Wie du auch strahlst in Diamantenpracht,
es fällt kein Strahl in deines Herzens Nacht,
das weiss ich längst.
Ich grolle nicht, und wenn das Herz auch bricht.
Ich sah dich ja im Traume,
und sah die Nacht in deines Herzens Raume,

ıç grɔllə nıçt ʊnt vɛn das hɛrts ɑox brıçt
evıç fɛrlɔrnəs lip ıç grɔlle nıçt
vi du ɑox ʃtralst ın diamantənpraxt
ɛs fɛlt kæn ʃtral ın dænəs hɛrtsəns naxt
das væs ıç lɛŋst
ıç grɔllə nıçt ʊnt vɛn das hɛrts ɑox brıçt
ıç za dıç ja ım traomə
ʊnt za di naxt ın dænəs hɛrtsəns raomə

und sah die Schlang', die dir am Herzen frisst,   ʊnt za di ʃlaŋ di dir am hɛrtsən frist

ich sah, mein Lieb, wie sehr du elend bist.   ɪç za mæn lip vi zer du elənt bɪst

Ich grolle nicht, ich grolle nicht.   ɪç grɔllə nɪçt ɪç grɔllə nɪçt

Allerseelen (All Souls' Day) – Richard Strauss

Richard Strauss (1864–1949) received early instruction in music from his father, a professional horn player. Richard had a symphony performed by the time he was seventeen and a second by the time he was twenty.

Richard Strauss was an accomplished conductor and composer, and this is one of his most beautiful songs. The vocal range is not taxing for a singer of some experience, but the line does require control of a wide dynamic range. The accompaniment, too, requires a capable pianist. The music begins with restraint and builds to a climactic point on "komm an mein Herz dass ich dich wieder habe." The last repetition of the closing "wie einst im Mai" is to be interpreted to portray an increasing sense of remembrance. The original key is said to be E flat.

Stell' auf den Tisch die duftenden Reseden,   ʃtel aof den tɪʃ di dʊftəndən rəzedən

die letzten roten Astern trag' herbei,   di lɛtstən rotən astərn trak hɛrbæ

und lass uns wieder von der Liebe reden,   ʊnt las ʊns vidər fɔn der libə redən

wie einst im Mai.   vi ænst ɪm mæ

Gib mir die Hand, dass ich sie heimlich drücke,   gip mir di hant das ɪç zi hæmlɪç drykə

und wenn man's sieht, mir ist es einerlei,   ʊnt vɛn mans zit mir ɪst es ænərlæ

gib mir nur einen deiner süssen Blicke,   gip mir nur ænən dænər zysən blɪkə

wie einst im Mai.   vi ænst ɪm mæ

Es blüht und duftet heut' auf jedem Grabe,   ɛs blyt ʊnt dʊftət hɔøt aof jedəm grabə

ein Tag im Jahr ist ja den Toten frei,   æn tak ɪm jar ɪst ja den totən fræ

komm an mein Herz, dass ich dich wieder habe   kɔm an mæn hɛrts das ɪç dɪç vidər habə

wie einst im Mai.   vi ænst ɪm mæ

FRENCH SONGS

Beau Soir (Evening Fair) – Debussy

Claude Debussy (1862–1918) studied at the Paris Conservatoire, and later went to Bayreuth and Rome where he heard the music of Wagner and the Italians. He has been classed, over his objection, as an impressionist, for he moved on from using traditional 19th century chords to also use the whole-tone scale and other less traditional techniques.

Debussy composed this song when he was fifteen or sixteen years old, and its original key is E major. Pierre Bernac states that a tempo of 72 quarter notes approximates the performance tempo. The character of this music is delicate rather than dramatic, and the textual expression concerns such thoughts as the setting sun, the joy of being alive, youth, and then departing from this world. The vocal range is not unusually wide, but this song should be sung by singers who are musically solid and technically capable. The singer must negotiate several rather difficult intervals smoothly and with restraint. But those singers who have no difficulty with the technical aspects of this song should find it enjoyable and rewarding to study. Indeed, it is among the French songs most often performed on recital programs.

Lorsqu'au soleil couchant les rivières sont roses,   lɔrsko sɔ lɛj kuʃɑ̃ le rivjɛrə sɔ̃ rozə

Et qu'un tiède frisson court sur les champs de blé.   e kœ̃ tjɛdə frisɔ̃ kur syr le ʃɑ̃ də ble

Un conseil d'être heureux semble sortir des choses   œ̃ kɔ̃sɛ jdə trørø sɑ̃blə sɔrti rde ʃozə

Et monter vers le coeur troublé   e mɔ̃te vɛ rlə kœr truble

Un conseil de goûter le charme d'être au monde
Cependant qu'on est jeune et que le soir est beau,
Car nous nous en allons, Comme s'en va cette onde;
Elle à la mer, Nous au tombeau.

œ̃ kɔ̃sɛ jdə gute lə ʃarmə dɛtro mɔ̃ də
səpãdã kɔ̃nɛ ʒœne kə lə swa rɛ bo
ka rnu nu zã nalɔ̃ kɔ̃mə sã va sɛ tɔ̃ də
ɛ la la mɛr nu o tɔ̃ bo

Romance – **Debussy**

Claude Debussy (1862–1918) studied at the Paris Conservatoire (1872–84) and in Rome (1885–87). He also visited Bayreuth (1889) and came to be influenced by Wagner. At times he also used such elements as church modes and the whole-tone scale in his compositions.

"Romance," originally in the key of D major, was composed in 1891. A tempo of 69 quarter notes has been suggested, but the tempo chosen should bring out the charm contained in the vocal line. It is recommended that the singer pronounce the final *s* of *lis* (lillies) and that the high optional notes near the end, when chosen for performance, be sung in one breath.

The pianist should initiate the *ritenuto* near the end and bring out the theme in its final statement; each succeeding note should be longer than the previous one. The singer is to continue in this attitude and finally take enough time to enunciate the last word *paix*, so as to evoke the final impression of peace.

L'âme évaporée et souffrante,
L'âme douce, l'âme odorante,
Des lis divins que j'ai cueillis
Dans le jardin de ta pensée,
Où donc les vents l'ont-ils chassée,
Cette âme adorable des lis?
N'est-il plus un parfum qui reste
De la suavité céleste,
Des jours où tu m'enveloppais
D'une vapeur surnaturelle,
Faite d'espoir, d'amour fidèle,
De béatitude et de paix?

lame vapɔre e sufrãtə
lamə du sə la mɔ dɔrãtə
de li sdivẽ kə ʒe kœji
dã lə ʒardẽ də ta pãse
u dɔ̃ kle vã lɔ̃ti lʃase
sɛ ta madɔrablə de lis
nɛ ti lply zœ̃ parfœ̃ ki rɛ stə
də la syavite se lɛstə
de ʒu ru ty mãvəlɔpɛ
dynə vapœɛ rsyrnatyrɛlə
fɛtə dɛspwar da mu rfidɛlə
də beatityd e də pɛ

Après un rêve (After a Dream) – **Fauré**

Gabriel Fauré (1845–1924), widely regarded as the master of French song, achieved recognition slowly. He taught at the Conservatoire in Paris, where his pupils included Maurice Ravel and Nadia Boulanger.

In "Après un rêve," the accompaniment is essentially an insistent succession of eighth-note chords in the right hand and octaves in the left. The singer must be able to execute triplets against the eighth-note chords in the accompaniment, for primary attention should be on the text. The first verse, in which the poet describes the image of his beloved as she appeared in a dream, should be sung rather softly in an attitude of happy remembrance. The second verse starts full and is more exalting: the beloved calls him and he leaves the earth to enjoy with her the splendors of heaven. In the third verse there is an abrupt change: the poet, awakening to find it all a dream, calls night to return with its marvelous deception. There should be no *ritard* at the end.

Dans un sommeil que charmait ton image,
Je rêvais le bonheur, ardent mirage;
Tes yeux étaient plus doux, ta voix pure et sonore.
Tu rayonnais comme un ciel éclairé par l'aurore;
Tu m'appelais, et je quittais la terre

dã zœ̃ sɔmɛ jkə ʃarmɛ tɔ̃ ni maʒə
ʒə rɛ ve lə bɔnœr ardã miraʒə
te zjøze tɛ ply du ta vwa pyre sɔnɔrə
tu rɛjɔne kɔmœ̃ sje le klɛre pa rlɔrɔrə
ty mapəlɛ e ʒə kitɛ la tɛrə

Pour m'enfuir avec toi vers la lumière;	pu rmɑ̃ fɥi rɑve ktwɑ vɛ rlɑ lymjɛrə
Les cieux pour nous entr'ouvraient leurs nues,	le sjø pu rnuzɑ̃tru vrɛ lœ rnyə
Splendeurs inconnues, lueurs divines entrevues...	splɑ̃dœ rzɛ̃ kɔnyə lyœ rdivinə zɑ̃trəvyə
Hélas! Hélas, triste réveil des songes!	elɑs elɑs tristə reve jde sɔ̃ʒə
Je t'appelle, ô nuit, rends-moi tes mensonges;	ʒə tɑpe lo nɥi rɑ̃mwɑ te mɑ̃sɔ̃ʒə
Reviens, reviens radieuse,	rəvjɛ̃ rəvjɛ̃ radiøzə
Reviens, ô nuit mystérieuse!	rəvjɛ̃ o nɥi misteriøzə

Obstination (A Resolve) – Fontenailles

Few French songs are so well suited to study and performance by beginners as this setting of a poem by François Coppée (1842–1902). The straightforward melodic line and steady syncopation in the accompaniment make this a very attractive song for study. The tempo of the first two verses should be kept moving rather briskly, with some relaxation near the end. But the *ritard* should be most noticeable at the close of verse three. Also, the tempo adopted for verse three may be a little slower than for verses one and two. The character of the music and rather narrow vocal range required of the singer make this song a traditional favorite for study and performance.

Vous aurez beau faire et beau dire;	vu zɔre bo fɛre bo dirə
L'oubli me serait odieux,	lubli mə səre todiø
Et je vois toujours son sourire	e ʒə vwɑ tuʒur sɔ̃ surirə
Des adieux, des adieux.	de zadjø de zadjø
Vous aurez beau faire et beau dire;	vu zɔre bo fɛr e bo dirə
Dût elle-même l'ignorer,	dyt ɛləmemə liɲɔre
Je veux, fidèle à mon martyre,	ʒə vø fidɛ lɑ mɔ̃ martirə
La pleurer, la pleurer.	lɑ plœre lɑ plœre
Vous aurez beau dire et beau faire,	vu zɔre bo dire bo fɛrə
Seule, elle peut mon mal guérir.	sœl ɛlə pø mɔ mɑl gerir
Et j'aime mieux s'il persévère	e ʒɛmə mjø s'il pɛrseverə
En mourir, en mourir.	ɑ̃ murir ɑ̃ murir

L'Heure exquise (The Exquisite Hour) – Hahn

Reynaldo Hahn (1874–1947) was a French composer of Venezuelan origin. He studied with Massenet at the Paris Conservatoire and was active as a composer and conductor.

This composition is surely his most performed art song. It contains a gentle motion in the accompaniment, the dynamics are always rather soft, and the singer must take care not to move too far toward either loudness or sentimentality. The text concerns love in the quietness of the night and is by the well-known poet Paul Verlaine (1844–1896).

If the performers take sufficient care to portray the true character of the music, the singer will be especially careful to communicate the meaning of the text and the quiet intimacy found in the music.

La lune blanche luit dans les bois;	lɑ lynə blɑ̃ʃə lɥi dɑ̃ le bwɑ
De chaque branche part une voix sous la ramée	də ʃɑkə brɑ̃ʃə pɑ ru nə vwɑ su lɑ rameə
ô bien aimée.	o bjɛ̃ nɛmeə
L'étang reflète, profond miroir	letɑ̃ rəfletə prɔfɔ̃mirwar
La silhouette du saule noir	lɑ s_luetə dy solə nwar
Où le vent pleure. Rêvons! c'est l'heure!...	u lə vɑ̃ plœrə rɛvɔ̃ sɛ lœrə
Un vaste et tendre apaisement semble descendre	œ̃ va ste tɑ̃ drɑ pɛzəmɑ̃ sɑ̃blə dɛsɑ̃drə
Du firmament que l'astre irise...	dy firmamɑ̃ kə lastri rizə
C'est l'heure exquise.	sɛ lœ rɛkskizə

Bois épais (Somber Woods) – Lully

Jean-Baptiste Lully (1632–1687) entered the service of Louis XIV when fourteen as a player in the royal string orchestra. He collaborated with the poet Quinault, and came to be credited as the founder of French opera. The opera *Amadis*, from which this aria is taken, is no longer performed, but this aria is in the standard repertory. It can be given to a student early in the study sequence, for it provides a singer with a very interesting melody and an opportunity to work toward a refined legato line. Also, this aria can serve as a fine vehicle for working to achieve refinement of breath control. A voice which is full and has a dark color will sound very well singing this music.

Performers should recognize that solo singers during the Baroque Era were expected to add ornamentation to the music already written down by the composer, and more experienced singers may wish to add their own ornamentation. Also, it should be understood that expression marks have been added by the editor.

Bois épais, redouble ton ombre;	bwɑ ze pɛ rədublə tɔ̃ nɔ̃brə
Tu ne saurais être assez sombre,	ty nə sɔrɛzɛ trɑse sɔ̃ brə
Tu ne peux trop cacher	ty nə pø tro kɑʃe
Mon malheureux amour.	mɔ̃ malørø zɑmur
Je sens un désespoir	ʒə sɑ̃ zœ̃ dezɛspwɑr
Dont l'horreur est extrême,	dɔ̃ lɔrœrɛ tɛkstrɛmə
Je ne dois plus voir ce que j'aime,	ʒə nə dwɑ ply vwɑ rsə kə ʒɛmə
Je ne veux plus souffrir le jour.	ʒə nə vø ply sufri rlə ʒur

LATIN SONGS

Libera me (Deliver Me, O Lord) – Fauré

This music was written for the baritone soloist in Fauré's *Requiem*. The music moves majestically, and the vocal range is one octave. This solo gives the singer an opportunity to study music with a Latin text while also performing mature music.

Gabriel Fauré (1845–1924) is placed near the close of the Romantic period and at the beginning of the 20th century. His contribution to the literature of French art song is without equal, and his style shows that he lived during a period of change. "Libera me" is colorful, and singers will enjoy singing with the required fullness of tone. It serves as an interesting solo taken from repertory for choral groups. (See "Pie Jesu" for additional information about Fauré.)

Libera me, Domine, de morte aeterna,	libera mɛ dɔminɛ dɛ mɔrtɛ ɛtɛrnɑ
in die illa tremenda:	in diɛ illɑ trɛmɛndɑ
Quando caeli movendi sunt et terra:	kwɑndɔ tʃɛli mɔvɛndi sunt ɛt tɛrrɑ
Dum veneris judicare saeculum per ignem.	dum vɛneris judikɑrɛ sɛkulum pɛr iɲɛm

Pie Jesu (Blessed Jesus) – Fauré

This music from Fauré's *Requiem* was composed for soprano soloist. The style of Gabriel Fauré (1845–1924) links him to the end of Romanticism and the early 20th century. Many elements of his individual style are rooted in the relationship of his handling of tonality and harmony. He has been called the greatest master of French art song, and his contribution to that literature is quite important. Fauré lived during a time when basic musical ideas were undergoing change; Berlioz was composing when Fauré was born, and Berg had just completed *Wozzeck* a few years before Fauré's death.

This music is conservative but colorful. It represents a literature not previously included in publications of song repertory, and it serves as an attractive example of solo music with a text in Latin.

Pie Jesu Domine, piɛ jɛzu dɔminɛ
dona eis requiem. Amen. dɔna ɛis rɛkwiɛm amɛn
dona eis requiem sempiternam. dɔna ɛis rɛkwiɛm sɛmpitɛrnam

Benedictus (excerpt from Mass in G) – Schubert

Franz Schubert (1797–1828) took violin lessons from his father and piano lessons from his brother. In 1808 Schubert was accepted as a chorister at the Imperial Chapel, and he composed his first song when he was fourteen years old.

Schubert is well known for his 600 art songs, symphonies, and many other compositions. He composed seven masses, of which "Mass in G" has been most often performed. The complete "Benedictus" was set for soprano, tenor, and baritone, and this excerpt includes that portion for the first two voices. It is lyrical music which should be sung by singers of some training and experience. While the complete roles for solo voices may prove to be more than some singers should attempt, this excerpt serves as an excellent example of music with Latin text. The text for the music included here can be translated as "Blessed is he who comes in the name of the Lord."

Benedictus qui venit in nomine Domini. bɛnɛdiktus kwi vɛnit in nɔminɛ dɔmini

Qui sedes ad dexteram (from Gloria) – Vivaldi

Antonio Vivaldi (1678–1741) was the son of a professional violinist who played at St. Mark's. Vivaldi trained for the priesthood and was ordained in 1703, but soon discontinued those duties because of illness. The same year, he was appointed *maestro di violino* at a Venetian orphanage for girls (Ospedale della Pietà); he continued there until 1709 and held the post again from 1711–16 when he became *maestro de' concerti*. He was *maestro di cappella* from 1735–38, and continued to conduct performances and supply concertos even after those years.

Vivaldi's reputation rests primarily with his instrumental music, which includes numerous trio sonatas, solo sonatas, and concertos. He was also quite active in the area of vocal music, for he composed many sacred works and operas.

Gloria continues to be an important work in the repertory of large choruses, and "Qui sedes ad dexteram" is sung by the contralto soloist. This music moves quickly, and the length of some phrases may be a problem for some singers. The text is conventional, and one writer has said that, although Vivaldi was a priest, there is nothing in this music to suggest that he took unusual care with this text.

Qui sedes ad dexteram Patris, kwi sɛdɛs ad dɛkstɛram patris
miserere nobis. mizɛrɛrɛ nɔbis

B *Pronunciation Chart*

Symbols from the International Phonetic Alphabet (IPA) used in the transcriptions

Vowel Sounds

IPA	English	French	Italian	German	Latin
[a]	pat	patte	—	—	—
[ɑ]	father	cadre	casa	Vater	ave
[ɑi]	mine	—	—	mein	—
[ɑʊ]	out	—	aura	auch	laudate
[ɑ̃]	—	enfant	—	—	—
[e]	take	école	chè	geben	—
[ɛ]	wed	pleine	menza	besser	et
[ɛi]	say	—	sei	—	mei
[ə]	sofa	le	—	Liebe	—
[ɛ̃]	—	pain	—	—	—
[i]	see	ici	si	lieber	tibi
[ɪ]	it	—	—	immer	—
[ɔ]	dog	ordinaire	dolce	Gott	dominus
[ɔi]	voice	—	poi	Leute	—
[o]	row	faux	tanto	Sohn	—
[õ]	—	ombre	—	—	—
[u]	rule	ou	tu	Blume	cum
[ʊ]	foot	—	—	Mutter	—
[y]	—	tu	—	glühen	—
[ø]	—	peu	—	—	—
[œ]	fern	peur	—	schön	—
[œ̃]	—	parfum	—	—	—

Additional information concerning pronunciation in English, French, German, and Italian may be found in Kenneth E. Miller, *Principles of Singing*, 2nd Edition, Prentice Hall, Englewood Cliffs, N.J., 1990, pp. 57-83.

Consonant Sounds

IPA	English	French	Italian	German	Latin
[b]	baby	bas	basso	bitte	beata
[ç]	—	—	—	ich	—
[d]	dead	détacher	dolce	du	dona
[f]	fear	fermer	felice	Vogel	filio
[g]	go	gloire	grande	gegen	ego
[h]	hat	—	—	Herz	—
[j]	yes	hier	ieri	Jahr	ejus
[k]	work	képi	che	Kraft	kyrie
[l]	love	la	lento	Lieb	lauda
[m]	may	madame	meno	mehr	Maria
[n]	noon	tenant	nome	nein	non
[ɲ]	onion	règne	ognuno	—	agnus
[ŋ]	sing	—	sangue	Ring	—
[p]	sleep	parole	padre	Paar	Pater
[r]	reed	triste	porta	rot	miserere
[s]	soon	savez	servo	das	sanctus
[ʃ]	sure	chiche	scena	Spiele	suscipe
[t]	not	table	terra	Tal	tanto
[v]	voice	vivre	veggo	warum	vero
[w]	watch	oui	guarda	—	qui
[x]	—	—	—	Nacht	—
[ʎ]	—	—	voglio	—	—
[z]	zoo	désire	rosa	Rose	Jesu
[ʒ]	measure	jour	—	Genie	—

Consonant Combinations

IPA	English	French	Italian	German	Latin
[dʒ]	George	—	gemo	—	Regina
[gz]	exert	exil	—	—	exsultate
[ks]	tacks	action	—	Sachs	dexteram
[kv]	—	—	—	Qual	—
[kw]	quick	—	questo	—	qui
[ts]	cats	—	senza	Spitz	gratia
[tʃ]	pitch	—	cielo	klatsch	coelo